INTEGRITY

TAKING ON TOUGH ISSUES

Serendipity House / P.O. Box 1012 / Littleton, CO 80160

TOLL FREE 1-800-525-9563 / www.serendipityhouse.com

01 02 03 04 / **201 series** • **CHG** / 9 8 7 6

PROJECT ENGINEER:
Lyman Coleman

WRITING TEAM:
Richard Peace, Lyman Coleman, Matthew Lockhart, Andrew Sloan, Cathy Tardif

PRODUCTION TEAM:
Christopher Werner, Sharon Penington, Erika Tiepel

COVER PHOTO:
© 1998 Ralph A. Clevenger/Westlight

CORE VALUES

Community:	The purpose of this curriculum is to build community within the body of believers around Jesus Christ.
Group Process:	To build community, the curriculum must be designed to take a group through a step-by-step process of sharing your story with one another.
Interactive Bible Study:	To share your "story," the approach to Scripture in the curriculum needs to be open-ended and right brain—to "level the playing field" and encourage everyone to share.
Developmental Stages:	To provide a healthy program in the life cycle of a group, the curriculum needs to offer courses on three levels of commitment: (1) Beginner Stage—low-level entry, high structure, to level the playing field; (2) Growth Stage—deeper Bible study, flexible structure, to encourage group accountability; (3) Discipleship Stage—in-depth Bible study, open structure, to move the group into high gear.
Target Audiences:	To build community throughout the culture of the church, the curriculum needs to be flexible, adaptable and transferable into the structure of the average church.

ACKNOWLEDGMENTS

To Zondervan Bible Publishers
for permission to use
the NIV text,
The Holy Bible, New International Bible Society.
© 1973, 1978, 1984 by International Bible Society.
Used by permission of Zondervan Bible Publishers.

Questions & Answers

STAGE

1. What stage in the life cycle of a small group is this course designed for?

Turn to the first page of the center section of this book. There you will see that this 201 course is designed for the second stage of a small group. In the Serendipity "Game Plan" for the multiplication of small groups, your group is in the Growth Stage.

GOALS

2. What are the goals of a 201 study course?

As shown on the second page of the center section (page M2), the focus in this second stage is equally balanced between Spiritual Formation, Group Building, and Mission / Multiplication.

BIBLE STUDY

201

3. What is the approach to Bible Study in this course?

Take a look at page M3 of the center section. The objective in a 201 course is to discover what a book of the Bible, or a series of related Scripture passages, has to say to our lives today. We will study each passage seriously, but with a strong emphasis on practical application to daily living.

FOUR-STAGE LIFE CYCLE OF A GROUP

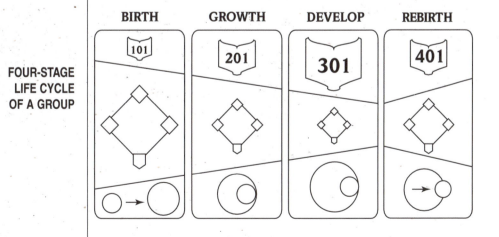

BIRTH · GROWTH · DEVELOP · REBIRTH

GROUP BUILDING

4. *What is the meaning of the baseball diamond on pages M2 and M3 in relation to Group Building?*

Every Serendipity course includes group building. First base is where we share our own stories; second base means affirming one another's stories; third base is sharing our personal needs; and home plate is deeply caring for each others' needs. In this 201 course we will continue "checking in" with each other and holding each other accountable to live the Christian life.

MISSION / MULTIPLICATION

5. *What is the mission of a 201 group?*

The mission of this 201 Covenant group is to discover the future leaders for starting a new group. (See graph on the previous page.) During this course, you will be challenged to identify three people and let this team use the Bible Study time to practice their skills. The center section will give you more details.

THE EMPTY CHAIR

6. *How do we fill "the empty chair"?*

First, pull up an empty chair during the group's prayer time and ask God to bring a new person to the group to fill it. Second, have everyone make a prospect list of people they could invite and keep this list on their refrigerator until they have contacted all those on their list.

AGENDA

7. *What is the agenda for our group meetings?*

A three-part agenda is found at the beginning of each session. Following the agenda and the recommended amount of time will keep your group on track and will keep the three goals of Spiritual Formation, Group Building, and Mission / Multiplication in balance.

SUBGROUPING

If you have nine or more people at a meeting, Serendipity recommends you divide into groups of 4–6 for the Bible Study. Count off around the group: "one, two, one, two, etc."—and have the "ones" move quickly to another room for the Bible Study. Ask one person to be the leader and follow the directions for the Bible Study time. After 30 minutes, the Group Leader will call "Time" and ask all subgroups to come together for the Caring Time.

ICE-BREAKERS

8. *How do we decide what ice-breakers to use to begin the meetings?*

Page M7 of the center section contains an index of ice-breakers in four categories: (1) those for getting acquainted in the first session or when a new person comes to a meeting; (2) those for the middle sessions to help you report in to your group; (3) those for the latter sessions to affirm each other and assign roles in preparation for starting a new group in the future; and (4) those for evaluating and reflecting in the final session.

GROUP COVENANT

9. *What is a group covenant?*

A group covenant is a "contract" that spells out your expectations and the ground rules for your group. It's very important that your group discuss these issues—preferably as part of the first session (also see page M32 in the center section).

GROUND RULES

10. *What are the ground rules for the group?* (Check those you agree upon.)

❒ PRIORITY: While you are in the course, you give the group meetings priority.

❒ PARTICIPATION: Everyone participates and no one dominates.

❒ RESPECT: Everyone is given the right to their own opinion and all questions are encouraged and respected.

❒ CONFIDENTIALITY: Anything that is said in the meeting is never repeated outside the meeting.

❒ EMPTY CHAIR: The group stays open to new people at every meeting.

❒ SUPPORT: Permission is given to call upon each other in time of need—even in the middle of the night.

❒ ADVICE GIVING: Unsolicited advice is not allowed.

❒ MISSION: We agree to do everything in our power to start a new group as our mission (see center section).

Introduction to 1 Corinthians

The City of Corinth

Corinth was an unusual city. After its capture by the Roman legions in 146 B.C., the city was leveled. It lay in waste for nearly 100 years until Julius Caesar rebuilt it in 44 B.C. Then it grew rapidly, thanks largely to its unique geographical location. Because it lay at the neck of a narrow isthmus connecting the two parts of Greece, it controlled all north-south land traffic. To the east and the west of the city were two fine harbors. Both goods and ships were hauled across the four-mile-wide Isthmus of Corinth. Thus Corinth also controlled most east-west sea routes. This strategic location commanded wealth and influence. By the time of Paul's visit some 100 years after its rebuilding, Corinth had become the capital of the province of Achaia and the third most important city in the Roman Empire, after Rome and Alexandria.

In this wealthy young city, excess seemed to be the norm. The city was stocked with art purchased from around the Roman Empire. It became a center of philosophy, though apparently few citizens were seriously interested in studying philosophy, preferring rather to listen to stirring orations on faddish topics delivered by the city's numerous itinerant philosophers. Even in religion, this excess was obvious. The Greek author Pausanias describes 26 pagan shrines and temples, including the great temples of Apollo and Aphrodite. In Old Corinth, 1,000 temple prostitutes had served Aphrodite, the goddess of love, and New Corinth continued this tradition of sexual worship practices. The city developed a worldwide reputation for vice and debauchery.

Luxury was the hallmark of Corinth. Because storms in the Aegean Sea were frequent and treacherous, sailors preferred to put into one of the harbors and transport their cargo to the other side by way of land—despite the exorbitant prices charged by the Corinthians. Consequently, goods from around the world passed through Corinthian ports, and some 400,000 slaves were kept in the city to provide the labor for this arduous job.

People from around the Roman Empire flowed into Corinth. There were "Greek adventurers and Roman bourgeois, with a tainting infusion of Phoenicians, a mass of Jews, ex-soldiers, philosophers, merchants, sailors, freed men, slaves, tradespeople, hucksters and agents of every form of vice" (Farrar, quoted by William Barclay, *The Letters to the Corinthians*, p. 4). Rootless, proud, independent, egalitarian, individualistic, rich—together the Corinthians shaped their new city into the cosmopolitan capital that it was in Paul's day. Not surprisingly, it was in Corinth that Paul had to fight this battle to prevent Christianity from succumbing to the debilitating enticements offered by paganism.

Paul and the Corinthians

Paul visited Corinth during his second missionary journey, probably in A.D. 50. Having been in some peril in Macedonia, he fled by ship to Athens (Acts 17:5–15). Not meeting with great success there (Acts 17:16–34), he then journeyed the short distance to Corinth, where he met Priscilla and Aquila (Acts 18:1–3). At first he preached in the synagogue with some success (even the ruler of the synagogue was won to Christ). But then the Jews forced him to leave, so he moved next door into the home of a Gentile. Hoping to silence him, the Jews eventually hauled Paul before the governor Gallio, but Gallio threw the case out of court as having no merit. After some 18 months (his longest stay anywhere except in Ephesus), Paul left and continued his missionary work in Syria.

There were two events that sparked the writing of 1 Corinthians some three or four years later. First, Paul heard that a divisive spirit was loose in the church (1 Cor. 1:11). Second, he received a letter in which the Corinthians asked him questions about marriage and other matters (1 Cor. 7:1). In addition, a delegation from Corinth completed his knowledge of the problems there (1 Cor. 16:15–17). Being unable to visit personally, Paul sought to deal with the issues by letter. Thus, the Corinthian correspondence was begun.

Theme

First Corinthians is a practical, issue-oriented letter in which Paul tells his readers what they ought or ought not to do. Paul's typical pattern in other letters is to begin with a strong theological statement and then to follow up by applying this insight to daily life. But this is not the case in 1 Corinthians. Here we find little direct theological teaching. Rather Paul discusses, in turn, a number of behavioral issues.

The problem was that these proud, materialistic, independent ex-pagans were having a most difficult time learning how to live as Christians. It was at this level of lifestyle that paganism directed its attack on the newly emerging Christian faith. *Christian behavior was the underlying issue.* Where were the lines to be drawn? How much of one's culture had to be abandoned to become a Christian? Residual paganism was mounting a frontal attack on Christianity. If Christianity lost in Corinth, its existence would be threatened throughout the Roman Empire. So just as he did in Galatians (when residual Judaism attacked Christianity over the issue of the Law), here in 1 Corinthians Paul struck back decisively and directly.

The Structure of 1 Corinthians

The problem in understanding 1 Corinthians is that we only have Paul's responses. We don't know with certainty what questions and problems he is addressing. These have to be deduced. Still, it is clear that there are two major divisions in the letter. In chapters 1–6, Paul responds to four problems of which he has become aware. Then, in chapters 7–15, he responds to a series of specific questions raised in a letter the Corinthians had sent him.

Outline

1. Problems Reported to Paul (1:10–6:20)

    A. Divisions in the Church (1:10–4:21)
    B. Incest (5:1–13)
    C. Lawsuits Among Believers (6:1–11)
    D. Sexual Immorality (6:12–20)

2. Questions Asked of Paul (7:1–15:58)

    A. Marriage (7:1–24)
    B. Virgins (7:25–40)
    C. Food Sacrificed to Idols (8:1–11:1)
    D. Propriety in Worship (11:2–34)
    E. Spiritual Gifts (12:1–14:40)
    F. The Resurrection (15:1–58)

In 1:1–9, Paul begins this letter in usual fashion; in chapter 16, he writes a concluding note.

The Church at Corinth

The membership of the Corinthian church reflected the diverse and cosmopolitan nature of the city itself. There were some Jews in the congregation, but it was mainly Gentile. There were some wealthy people, but most were working-class people including slaves. Despite these differences, they did share some things in common. They all had been influenced by the permissive, pagan atmosphere of the city. They were not necessarily great intellectuals, but they were very fond of "wisdom," and "knowledge" and came to pride themselves in their possession of it. They were all much taken with the so-called "supernatural" gifts of the Holy Spirit—like speaking in tongues, prophesying, and so forth.

This was not a group that probably would

have been drawn together in the normal course of affairs, except for the fact that they had met Jesus and he had changed their lives. They didn't know a lot about Jesus yet, and when it came to lifestyle they certainly muddled Christianity and culture together. With God's grace, Paul's instruction and the Holy Spirit's power, they would learn and grow.

PAUL'S JOURNEY FROM ANTIOCH TO CORINTH

1 Opening Remarks—1 Cor. 1:1–17

THREE-PART AGENDA

ICE-BREAKER
15 Minutes

BIBLE STUDY
30 Minutes

CARING TIME
15–45 Minutes

> *LEADER: Be sure to read pages 3–5 in the front of this book, and go over the ground rules on page 5 with the group in this first session. See page M7 in the center section for a good ice-breaker. Have your group look at pages M1–M5 in the center section and fill out the team roster on page M5.*

TO BEGIN THE BIBLE STUDY TIME
(Choose 1 or 2)

1. When you were 8 years old, who was your hero?

2. Growing up, who did you quarrel with the most? Over what?

3. What are you thankful for about your church?

READ SCRIPTURE & DISCUSS
(If you don't have time for all the questions in this section, conclude the Bible Study [30 min.] by answering question #7.)

1. Who is someone you've tried to model your life after?

2. From reading verses 4–9, what impression do you get of the Corinthians? What do the people in your community have in common with the Corinthians?

3. What was causing the quarrels among the Corinthians (see notes on v. 12)? How big of an issue has this been in your church? How has this affected you personally?

4. Why are cliques and divisions in the church so damaging?

1 Paul, called to be an apostle of Christ Jesus by the will of God, and our brother Sosthenes,

²To the church of God in Corinth, to those sanctified in Christ Jesus and called to be holy, together with all those everywhere who call on the name of our Lord Jesus Christ—their Lord and ours:

³Grace and peace to you from God our Father and the Lord Jesus Christ.

Thanksgiving

⁴I always thank God for you because of his grace given you in Christ Jesus. ⁵For in him you have been enriched in every way—in all your speaking and in all your knowledge— ⁶because our testimony about Christ was confirmed in you. ⁷Therefore you do not lack any spiritual gift as you eagerly wait for our Lord Jesus Christ to be revealed. ⁸He will keep you strong to the end, so that you will be blameless on the day of our Lord Jesus Christ. ⁹God, who has called you into fellowship with his Son Jesus Christ our Lord, is faithful.

Divisions in the Church

¹⁰I appeal to you, brothers, in the name of our Lord Jesus Christ, that all of you agree with one another so that there may be no divisions among you and that you may be perfectly united in mind and thought. ¹¹My brothers, some from Chloe's household have informed me that there are quarrels among you. ¹²What I mean is this: One of you says, "I follow Paul"; another, "I follow Apollos"; another, "I follow Cephas";ᵃ still another, "I follow Christ."

¹³Is Christ divided? Was Paul crucified for you? Were you baptized intoᵇ the name of Paul? ¹⁴I am thankful that I did not baptize any of you except Crispus and Gaius, ¹⁵so no one can say that you were baptized into my name. ¹⁶(Yes, I also baptized the household of Stephanas; beyond that, I don't remember if I baptized anyone else.) ¹⁷For Christ did not send me to baptize, but to preach the gospel—not with words of human wisdom, lest the cross of Christ be emptied of its power.

ᵃ12 That is, Peter.   ᵇ13 Or in; also in verse 15

5. What grade would you give your church right now on being "united in mind and thought" (v. 10)?

6. On a scale of 1 (far) to 10 (near), how close do you feel to Christ right now?

7. What brought you to this study and what are you hoping to get out of it?

CARING TIME

1. Has your group agreed on its group covenant and ground rules (see page 5 in the front of this book)?

2. Have you filled out your team roster (see page M5 in the center section)? Like any winning team, every position needs to be covered.

3. Who is someone you would like to invite to this group for next week?

Share prayer requests and close in prayer. Be sure to pray for "the empty chair" (see p. 4).

1:1–9 Paul begins this letter in conventional Greek fashion. Paul must face some very difficult issues in this letter. But rather than plunging right in with a spirit of judgment and a list of rules, he begins with thanksgiving. Whatever irregularities might exist at Corinth, they do so in the context of the good work that God has done in their midst.

1:1 *an apostle.* Paul does not always identify himself by this title (e.g., 1 Thess. 1:1). He may do so here because his authority as an apostle is an issue with the Corinthians. An apostle is "one who is sent," "an envoy." It is an office held by those who witnessed the resurrected Christ and were called by Christ to this position. Their special job was to plant new churches throughout the Roman Empire.

by the will of God. Paul did not just decide that he would like to be an apostle and so proclaim himself one. God made it quite clear that he had chosen Paul for this task (Acts 22:21).

our brother. Sosthenes is not an apostle. He is, however, a son of God the Father and thus part of God's family (as are all Christians). That is the basis on which Christians are meant to relate to one another—as kin, with sharing, care and patient love.

> *Grace is the unmerited gift of God by which a person comes into salvation. Peace is the outcome of that salvation, and has the idea of "wholeness" and "health."*

Sosthenes. It is possible that this is the same Sosthenes from Acts 18:17.

1:2 *sanctified.* Consecrated, dedicated to the service of God.

called. In the same way that Paul was called to be an apostle (v. 1), every believer is called by God to be holy.

holy. To be set apart to serve God's purposes, in much the same fashion as in the Old Testament where priests were set apart to serve a special religious function. In the New Testament all believers are "saints" (i.e., holy persons).

1:3 *Grace and peace.* Grace is the unmerited gift of God by which a person comes into salvation. Peace is the outcome of that salvation, and has the idea of "wholeness" and "health."

1:5 *in every way.* Gifts of grace include salvation itself (v. 2), special supernatural gifts (v. 5), and acquittal on the Day of Judgment (v. 8).

all your speaking. Probably a reference to the gift of tongues (12:10), to prophecy (14:1), to messages of wisdom and knowledge (12:8), etc. In Corinth, the oratory of philosophers was common and valued. As part of their riches in Christ, the Christians too, it seems, had been given various speech-related abilities. This, however, led to problems in the church which Paul deals with in this letter.

knowledge. The ability to understand and apply Christian truth. Their knowledge, while undoubtedly real and a gift of grace, had also led to problems. Paul is grateful for the very thing that has gone astray!

1:7 *you do not lack any spiritual gift.* This is said both seriously (since Christians have at their disposal all of God's grace-gifts) and tongue-in-cheek (as Paul echoes their own boasting). In fact, "the troubles in Corinth were due not to a deficiency of gifts but to lack of proportion and balance in estimating and using them" (Barrett).

spiritual gift. Charismata, Paul's word for the special gifts given by God, such as the gift of healing or of speaking in tongues. These gifts had a special fascination for the Corinthians. They serve as direct witnesses to the supernatural nature of Christianity. They spring from the general fact of grace (v. 4) and are specific examples of the operation of God's grace.

to be revealed. Christians live in eager expectation until Christ returns and ushers in the new kingdom. Meanwhile, the gifts of God are a foretaste of what one day will be normative.

1:8 *blameless.* Christians need not fear judgment since Jesus himself has already secured their acquittal by his death.

1:10–17 The first problem that Paul deals with is divisions in the church. It seems that the

Corinthians had begun to view Christianity as a new philosophy ("wisdom"), and the apostles were regarded (and judged) as if they were itinerant philosophers. After defining the problem (1:10–12), Paul launches into an explanation of divine wisdom (1:13–2:16). Then, after a transition paragraph (3:1–4), he points out that Christian teachers are all servants of the same God, not philosophers competing with one another for an audience (3:5–4:21).

> **Christians need not fear judgment since Jesus himself has already secured their acquittal by his death.**

1:10 *I appeal to you.* "I beg you, I beseech you." This matter of their divisions is serious and must be dealt with.

brothers. This is the basis of his appeal. Paul can write this way because they are all related to one another. It is not merely a matter of belonging to the same organization. They are part of the same family.

agree with one another. "Make up your differences," "let go of your party slogans."

divisions. *Schismata* (from which the English word "schisms" comes); a word often used to describe tears in a piece of clothing.

united in mind and thought. Their disunity is rooted in differing ideas (doctrines). To be restored, to knit back together the church which is torn apart, requires a unity of understanding.

1:11 *Chloe's household.* Paul is writing from Ephesus. The slaves (or freedmen) of an Ephesian woman named Chloe had visited the church in Corinth and brought back the story of the disunity there.

1:12 It is important to notice these slogans because they are the first of a series of slogans to which Paul must respond (e.g., see 6:12 and 7:1). Various Christian leaders unwittingly have become rallying points for dissension.

I follow Paul. Paul does not commend those "on his side." A faction in his name is no better than any other faction. In fact, these folks had probably exaggerated and falsified his actual viewpoints. (This was probably the Gentile party.)

I follow Apollos. After he had been instructed in the Gospel by Priscilla and Aquila, Apollos went to Corinth to assist the church there. A bright, articulate Jew from Alexandria with great skill in debate (see Acts 18:24–28) would be a natural leader for those who attempted to intellectualize Christianity.

I follow Cephas. Cephas is the Jewish form of the name Peter. It is probable that Peter also visited Corinth. This faction probably would have been oriented toward a more Jewish Christianity.

I follow Christ. These are possibly the people who look with disdain on the other groups who profess allegiance to the Christ preached by Paul, by Apollos, or by Cephas. Instead, they profess allegiance to the Christ they know without the teaching of anyone. This may even be a mystical or gnostic-like party, given to inner visions and revelations.

1:13 Paul makes his point by asking three rhetorical questions, the answer to each being clearly "No."

1:14–17a Paul is not belittling baptism. His point is simply that it does not matter who baptized a person, since all baptized people belong to Christ alone.

1:17b Here Paul comes to the principle that lies at the root of the problem in Corinth. They can form such factions only because they misunderstand the nature of God's wisdom.

wisdom. *Sophia*, a key word in 1 Corinthians, which Paul uses in both positive and negative ways. Here the idea is negative. This is wisdom defined as the skillful use of human reason with a view to convincing the hearer of the truth of a position.

lest the cross of Christ be emptied. That is, lest it "dwindle to nothing, vanish under the weight of rhetorical argument and dialectic subtlety" (Lightfoot). Paul is eager that people be persuaded by Christ crucified and not by mere eloquence.

2 True Wisdom—1 Cor. 1:18–2:5

THREE-PART AGENDA

ICE-BREAKER
15 Minutes

BIBLE STUDY
30 Minutes

CARING TIME
15–45 Minutes

LEADER: If there's a new person in your group in this session, start with an ice-breaker (see page M7 in the center section). Then begin the session with a word of prayer. If you have more than nine in your group, see the box about the "Subgrouping" on page 4. Count off around the group: "one, two, one, two, etc."—and have the "ones" move quickly to another room for the Bible Study.

TO BEGIN THE BIBLE STUDY TIME
(Choose 1 or 2)

1. What was more important to you in high school—getting good grades or having fun?

2. If you could boast about one thing regarding yourself or your family, what would it be?

3. Would you rather go to the dentist or give a speech? When was the last time you had to speak in public?

READ SCRIPTURE & DISCUSS
(If you don't have time for all the questions in this section, conclude the Bible Study [30 min.] by answering question #7.)

1. What was your best subject in school? Your worst?

2. How does the world define wisdom? How has "God made foolish the wisdom of the world" (v. 20)?

3. How does this passage illustrate that God's ways are not our ways?

Christ the Wisdom and Power of God

¹⁸For the message of the cross is foolishness to those who are perishing, but to us who are being saved it is the power of God. ¹⁹For it is written:

"I will destroy the wisdom of the wise;
the intelligence of the intelligent I will frustrate."

²⁰Where is the wise man? Where is the scholar? Where is the philosopher of this age? Has not God made foolish the wisdom of the world? ²¹For since in the wisdom of God the world through its wisdom did not know him, God was pleased through the foolishness of what was preached to save those who believe. ²²Jews demand miraculous signs and Greeks look for wisdom, ²³but we preach Christ crucified: a stumbling block to Jews and foolishness to Gentiles, ²⁴but to those whom God has called, both Jews and Greeks, Christ the power of God and the wisdom of God. ²⁵For the foolishness of God is wiser than man's wisdom, and the weakness of God is stronger than man's strength.

²⁶Brothers, think of what you were when you were called. Not many of you were wise by human standards; not many were influential; not many were of noble birth. ²⁷But God chose the foolish things of the world to shame the wise; God chose the weak things of the world to shame the strong. ²⁸He chose the lowly things of this world and the despised things—and the things that are not—to nullify the things that are, ²⁹so that no one may boast before him. ³⁰It is because of him that you are in Christ Jesus, who has become for us wisdom from God—that is, our righteousness, holiness and redemption. ³¹Therefore, as it is written: "Let him who boasts boast in the Lord."

2 *When I came to you, brothers, I did not come with eloquence or superior wisdom as I proclaimed to you the testimony about God. ²For I resolved to know nothing while I was with you except Jesus Christ and him crucified. ³I came to you in weakness and fear, and with much trembling. ⁴My message and my preaching were not with wise and persuasive words, but with a demonstration of the Spirit's power, ⁵so that your faith might not rest on men's wisdom, but on God's power.*

4. Why did God choose the foolish, weak and lowly things of the world (vv. 27–28)? In what ways have you seen God use these type of people?

5. What does this passage say to you about the wisdom of God versus worldly wisdom?

6. What does Paul mean when he says the message of the cross is foolish to some and powerful to others (v. 18)? What has the message of the cross meant in your life?

7. What issue or decision are you facing right now for which you need God's wisdom?

CARING TIME

(Choose 1 or 2 of these questions before closing in prayer. Be sure to pray for the empty chair.)

1. If you were to describe this past week in your life in terms of weather, how was it: Sunny and warm? Cold and rainy? Stormy? Other? What is the forecast for this next week?

2. How do you feel sharing about your spiritual life and struggles with this group?

3. How can the group pray for you this week?

Summary. The fact that the Corinthians can boast of party slogans is a clear indication that they over-value human wisdom and misunderstand the nature of the Gospel. Paul shows that the Gospel is decidedly not a species of human philosophy—because it involves such a reversal of human expectation. Who would have thought that God would work through the scandal of the cross? Only God could demonstrate his power through a dying, powerless "criminal." Paul then goes on to "prove" that God does indeed work through weakness. He first looks at the Corinthians (1:26–31) and then at himself (2:1–5), pointing out that they were not very clever and he was not very persuasive, so the fact they are Christians "proves" that God works through weakness. How else could the fact of the church at Corinth be explained?

1:18 *the message of the cross.* This is the only legitimate slogan. Paul puts the issue in stark terms: the question of eternal destiny centers on the meaning of the Cross. Their misunderstanding and division is no slight matter. It strikes at the core of the Gospel.

foolishness. It is absurd to many that God's redemptive activity involves death by crucifixion.

perishing. Unless they repent (turn around and go the other way), they will not be acquitted on the Day of Judgment.

being saved. Salvation is a process, begun at conversion, consummated at the Second Coming, and fulfilled in the New Age.

1:19 Paul quotes Isaiah 29:14 to demonstrate that human-centered wisdom will be overthrown by God.

1:20 All those who represent human wisdom are forced to flee in the face of God's revelation that their wisdom is actually mere folly.

1:22 *Jews demand miraculous signs.* The Jews expected a Messiah who would come in obvious power doing miraculous deeds. In Jesus they saw one so weak that his enemies got away with killing him. "To the Jew, a crucified Messiah was an impossible contradiction, like 'cooked ice' " (Fee). The Jews demanded that God certify his activity by means of supernatural acts.

Greeks look for wisdom. Their delight was in clever, cunning logic delivered with soaring persua-siveness. That a Jewish peasant who died as a convicted criminal could be the focus of God's redemptive plan was so silly to them as to be laughable.

1:23 To accept the Cross is to accept that people cannot understand God on their own nor find ways to reach him by themselves. They must trust God, not human wisdom and power. This is scandalous to many.

> *God chooses the "nobodies" and thus exposes the foolishness of the way the world defines the "somebodies."*

stumbling block. Literally, a scandal. Jesus' crucifixion "proved" to the Jews that he could not be of God (since Deut. 21:23 says those hanging from a tree are cursed of God). A suffering, dying Messiah was totally outside first-century Jewish expectations.

foolishness. Both the Incarnation and Crucifixion were actions Greeks felt were unworthy of their gods. In fact, the cradle and the cross show that people cannot reach God via the route of power, wisdom or reason, but only by the response of faith to that which has been done for them.

1:24 In fact, Christ is both the sign that is craved by the Jews (he's the power of God) and the ultimate truth desired by the Greeks (he's the wisdom of God).

1:25 There is indeed a paradox at the heart of the Gospel, at least when the Gospel is viewed through the lens of human wisdom. For in actual fact, Christ crucified conveys the truth about God and provides the power to break human bondage.

1:26 *think of what you were.* In their own calling they see the paradox of the all-powerful God using the "weak things of the world."

Not many. The early church had special appeal to the poor and to those with little social standing. This was part of its offensiveness—the "wrong" people were attracted to it. On the other hand, it is clear that there were some influential people in the Corinthian Church. For example, there was Crispus, a former head of the synagogue who had a position of status in the Jewish community (Acts 18:8), and there was Erastus, who as director of public works in Corinth, was a man of wealth and power (Rom. 16:23b).

wise. This refers to people with education or philosophical training.

> *It is by Christ's redeeming work on the cross that wisdom, righteousness and holiness are mediated to humankind.*

influential. This means people in high positions politically or socially.

noble birth. These were people of distinguished families who may have held Roman citizenship.

1:27 the foolish things of the world. Those who in the estimation of the current culture were insignificant.

to shame. The calling of the insignificant shows that the opinions of the "wise" about the worth of certain people or about how one approached God were wrong.

1:28 the things that are not / the things that are. God chooses the "nobodies" and thus exposes the foolishness of the way the world defines the "somebodies."

1:29 A church composed of such folk ought to have a better grasp of what the Gospel is all about, because they would know that it was not on account of who they were or what they had done that they were chosen. There ought to be, therefore, no false boasting within the church. To boast is to wrongly evaluate one's own gifts, to put confidence in them, and to express this with a tinge of pride. Such boasting, however, was one of the problems in the Corinthian church.

1:30 because of him. They owe the fact that they are related to God solely to Jesus Christ.

wisdom from God. Paul spoke of "human wisdom" in 1:17, i.e., philosophical wisdom. Here he begins to "de-philosophize" *sophia* (wisdom) and instead

historicize it. The historical Jesus is God's wisdom. It is Christ who mediates God's plan of salvation.

righteousness. Christ is their righteousness in that he took upon himself the guilt of human sin. So on the Last Day when Christians stand before the Judge, they are viewed not in terms of their own failure and inadequacy but as being "in Christ."

holiness. Human beings cannot come before a Holy God because they are not holy; but once again, Christ provides what people lack. His holiness suffices for them and a relationship with God is assured.

redemption. It is by Christ's redeeming work on the cross that wisdom, righteousness and holiness are mediated to humankind.

1:31 Here Paul quotes Jeremiah 9:24.

2:1–5 Paul shows that his own ministry amongst them was a demonstration of the principles outlined in 1:18–31.

2:1 eloquence or superior wisdom. "The two nouns are close together in meaning, for *eloquence* (literally, *logos* or 'word') here is rational talk, and wisdom worldly cleverness. They represent the outward and inward means by which men may commend a case, effectiveness of language, and skill of argumentation" (Barrett).

2:2 In Corinth, a city teeming with articulate philosophers, Paul's refusal to make persuasive speech and brilliant logic preeminent in his evangelism was especially striking. Instead, he simply told of the crucified Christ, "the most scandalous feature of the Christian message."

2:3 This weakness and fear was not for his safety, but due to Paul's sense of the awesome responsibility he had as a preacher of the Gospel (2 Cor. 2:16).

2:4 Paul says he was not an impressive speaker (2 Cor. 10:1), even though his writing (which often has the "feel" of speech) is often quite eloquent (e.g., Rom. 8 and 1 Cor. 13).

demonstration of the Spirit's power. Paul reveals the secret behind the impact that his preaching made. People were moved by the convicting power of the Holy Spirit. This is the real proof of the validity of the Gospel.

3 The Spirit's Wisdom—1 Cor. 2:6–16

THREE-PART AGENDA

ICE-BREAKER	BIBLE STUDY	CARING TIME
15 Minutes	30 Minutes	15–45 Minutes

> **LEADER:** *If there's a new person in your group in this session, start with an ice-breaker (see page M7 in the center section). Then begin the session with a word of prayer. If you're following the 12-week study plan, allow 60 minutes for the Bible Study time, as you are covering questions from two sessions. Follow the usual agenda for the Ice-Breaker and Caring Time, choosing those questions from either session.*

TO BEGIN THE BIBLE STUDY TIME
(Choose 1 or 2)

1. What did you want to be when you were 12 years old?

2. What foreign language can you speak (or understand) or would like to?

3. If you could ask God for the answer to any mystery of the universe, what would you ask?

READ SCRIPTURE & DISCUSS
(If you don't have time for all the questions in this section, conclude the Bible Study [30 min.] by answering question #7.)

1. Who do you turn to when you need some wisdom: Your spouse? A parent? Your pastor? A friend? Other?

2. What does Paul mean by God's "secret wisdom" (see notes on v. 7)?

3. From this passage, what role do you see the Holy Spirit playing in the life of a believer?

Wisdom From the Spirit

⁶We do, however, speak a message of wisdom among the mature, but not the wisdom of this age or of the rulers of this age, who are coming to nothing. ⁷No, we speak of God's secret wisdom, a wisdom that has been hidden and that God destined for our glory before time began. ⁸None of the rulers of this age understood it, for if they had, they would not have crucified the Lord of glory. ⁹However, as it is written:

> *"No eye has seen,*
>   *no ear has heard,*
> *no mind has conceived*
>   *what God has prepared for those who love*
>   *him"*ᵃ—

¹⁰but God has revealed it to us by his Spirit.

*The Spirit searches all things, even the deep things of God. ¹¹For who among men knows the thoughts of a man except the man's spirit within him? In the same way no one knows the thoughts of God except the Spirit of God. ¹²We have not received the spirit of the world but the Spirit who is from God, that we may understand what God has freely given us. ¹³This is what we speak, not in words taught us by human wisdom but in words taught by the Spirit, expressing spiritual truths in spiritual words.*ᵇ *¹⁴The man without the Spirit does not accept the things that come from the Spirit of God, for they are foolishness to him, and he cannot understand them, because they are spiritually discerned. ¹⁵The spiritual man makes judgments about all things, but he himself is not subject to any man's judgment:*

> *¹⁶"For who has known the mind of the Lord*
>   *that he may instruct him?"*ᶜ

But we have the mind of Christ.

ᵃ9 Isaiah 64:4   ᵇ13 Or *Spirit, interpreting spiritual truths to spiritual men*   ᶜ16 Isaiah 40:13

4. According to verse 14, who can't understand the things of God and why?

5. In practical terms, what does it mean to you to have "the mind of Christ" (v. 16)?

6. When in your spiritual journey did the "mind of Christ" start to make a difference in your values, choices and decisions?

7. Where do you need the guidance of God's Spirit most in your life for this coming week?

CARING TIME
(Choose 1 or 2 of these questions before closing in prayer. Be sure to pray for the empty chair.)

1. Who can you add to your "prospect list" to invite to this group?

2. Share with the group something for which you are particularly thankful.

3. How can the group help you in prayer this week?

Summary. Paul will now qualify what he just said about his rejection of human wisdom (2:4–5). There is, in fact, a legitimate "message of wisdom"; but, as he shows in verses 6–16, it comes from God and is discerned only by those who have the Spirit.

2:6 *a message of wisdom.* Paul will now use *sophia* (wisdom) in a positive way to describe God's plan of salvation. This use of *sophia* stands in sharp contrast to that in 1:17 (see note), where wisdom is seen as persuasive human eloquence (and to the uses in 1:18–25, where wisdom is evil because it makes human aspiration the criterion for truth).

among. Paul did not speak as some sort of elevated leader with insight no one else had. Rather the "message of wisdom" was shared in the context of the insights of other mature Christians who also had something to add (1 Cor. 12:8).

mature. To be mature is to be a full-grown adult in the faith, a potential which all Christians have (see Col. 1:28) though not all experience (1 Cor. 3:1).

but not. Paul first describes what God's wisdom is not: it is not derived from either the self-serving philosophy of fallen men and women, nor from the presuppositions of the rulers.

wisdom of this age. In biblical thought there are two ages: "this age" in which sin and evil exist, and "the age to come" when God's kingdom will be present and visible. Wisdom of this age is person-centered and corrupted by rebellion against God, despite how it may appear on the surface.

> *To be mature is to be a full-grown adult in the faith, a potential which all Christians have though not all experience.*

rulers of this age. Sometimes this term is used to describe evil supernatural powers thought to control human destiny, but here it seems Paul is referring to human leaders (since in verse 8 he says that these are the ones who crucified Jesus). The contrast in this whole passage is between the Christian (who has the Spirit) and the non-Christian (who does not).

2:7 *God's secret wisdom.* In contrast to the "wisdom of the world" (in which the attempt is made to show by persuasive words of rhetoric how "obvious" and "reasonable" it is), no one could have guessed God's plan. Even when it was revealed, many shunned it as "foolish" and/or scandalous (1:23).

> *It is not education or intellect or occupation that yields spiritual insight. There is only one source: the Holy Spirit dwelling within a believer.*

secret. This is not a secret (literally, "mystery"), in the sense of something that is cryptic and beyond human understanding. Rather, it means something God alone knew (it was once hidden) but which he has now revealed.

hidden. To be understood in the sense God's plan of salvation was only just recently disclosed (Paul is writing some 20–30 years after the Crucifixion) via the death and resurrection of Jesus, prior to which God's full intentions were known by no one.

destined for our glory. God always intended that humanity be redeemed and become a part of his glorious kingdom.

2:8 *understood.* No one understood that Christ crucified was to be God's agent of redemption.

2:9 Paul quotes Isaiah 64:4 as an example of how God's plan has always been a surprise to people.

2:10 *revealed it to us.* That which was hidden from the non-Christian rulers (v. 8) has now been made clear to the Christian.

by his Spirit. The insight referred to in verses 6–9 came not as a result of reasoning but as a result of revelation.

The Spirit searches all things. In Corinth, the idea was that you could (by means of philosophy) search out the nature of God. Paul indicates that only the Spirit himself knows and communicates accurate knowledge about God.

> **The Spirit provides both understanding and the very "language that makes conversation about these truths possible."**

2:11 Paul uses an analogy to make his point.

2:12 *the spirit of the world.* An equivalent phrase to "the wisdom of this age" (v. 6).

understand. It is not education or intellect or occupation that yields spiritual insight. There is only one source: the Holy Spirit dwelling within a believer.

has freely given us. These gifts of God (v. 9) are not merely for the future, but are the present experience of Christians.

2:13 The Spirit provides both understanding ("inward apprehension of profound divine truths"—v. 12) and the very "language that makes conversation about these truths possible" (Barrett).

we. Not just Paul and his coworkers, but probably all mature Christians (v. 6) have this experience—or at least the potential for it.

2:14 *The man without the Spirit.* In contrast to the spirit-filled person in verse 12 is the person who lacks the Holy Spirit and therefore is blind to the spiritual side of life.

2:15 *judgments.* Not only does the Holy Spirit give understanding, but he provides a moral standard by which to evaluate all things.

subject to any man's judgment. Barrett suggests that what Paul means here is similar to what he says in 4:3–5: "human condemnation or acquittal are nothing to him. His only judge is the Lord."

2:16 *mind of Christ.* Although Isaiah 40:13 was originally intended to show that no one could know God's thoughts, Paul declares that through the Gospel the mind of the Lord is indeed known by his people. This parallels the idea of having the Spirit of God (v. 12).

"The Buried Life"

But often, in the world's most crowded streets,
But often, in the din of strife,
There rises an unspeakable desire
After the knowledge of our buried life:
A thirst to spend our fire and restless force
In tracking out our true, original course;
A longing to inquire
Into the mystery of this heart which beats
So wild, so deep in us—to know
Whence our lives come and where they go.

Matthew Arnold

> **Not only does the Holy Spirit give understanding, but he provides a moral standard by which to evaluate all things.**

4 One Foundation—1 Cor. 3:1–23

THREE-PART AGENDA

ICE-BREAKER	**BIBLE STUDY**	**CARING TIME**
15 Minutes	30 Minutes	15–45 Minutes

 LEADER: Check page M7 in the center section for a good ice-breaker, particularly if you have a new person at this meeting. Is your group working well together—with everyone "fielding their position" as shown on the team roster on page M5?

TO BEGIN THE BIBLE STUDY TIME
(Choose 1 or 2)

1. How are you at growing things? Building things?

2. In junior high school, who was someone you were jealous of and why?

3. Looking back, at what age would you say you became a "grown-up"?

READ SCRIPTURE & DISCUSS
(If you don't have time for all the questions in this section, conclude the Bible Study [30 min.] by answering question #7.)

1. In your observation, what issues are most likely to cause division within a church?

2. What problems tend to cause strife at your work? In your home? In your community?

3. From this passage, what are the characteristics of worldly versus spiritual people?

4. From verses 6–9, who plants? Who waters? Who is the field? Who is responsible for growth? How does this illustration relate to the problem in the Corinthian church?

On Divisions in the Church

3 Brothers, I could not address you as spiritual but as worldly—mere infants in Christ. [2]I gave you milk, not solid food, for you were not yet ready for it. Indeed, you are still not ready. [3]You are still worldly. For since there is jealousy and quarreling among you, are you not worldly? Are you not acting like mere men? [4]For when one says, "I follow Paul," and another, "I follow Apollos," are you not mere men?

[5]What, after all, is Apollos? And what is Paul? Only servants, through whom you came to believe—as the Lord has assigned to each his task. [6]I planted the seed, Apollos watered it, but God made it grow. [7]So neither he who plants nor he who waters is anything, but only God, who makes things grow. [8]The man who plants and the man who waters have one purpose, and each will be rewarded according to his own labor. [9]For we are God's fellow workers; you are God's field, God's building.

[10]By the grace God has given me, I laid a foundation as an expert builder, and someone else is building on it. But each one should be careful how he builds. [11]For no one can lay any foundation other than the one already laid, which is Jesus Christ. [12]If any man builds on this foundation using gold, silver, costly stones, wood, hay or straw, [13]his work will be shown for what it is, because the Day will bring it to light. It will be revealed with fire, and the fire will test the quality of each man's work. [14]If what he has built survives, he will receive his reward. [15]If it is burned up, he will suffer loss; he himself will be saved, but only as one escaping through the flames.

[16]Don't you know that you yourselves are God's temple and that God's Spirit lives in you? [17]If anyone destroys God's temple, God will destroy him; for God's temple is sacred, and you are that temple.

[18]Do not deceive yourselves. If any one of you thinks he is wise by the standards of this age, he should become a "fool" so that he may become wise. [19]For the wisdom of this world is foolishness in God's sight. As it is written: "He catches the wise in their craftiness"[a]; [20]and again, "The Lord knows that the thoughts of the wise are futile."[b] [21]So then, no more boasting about men! All things are yours,

5. Who are the people that God has used in your life—the "Paul" who planted and the "Apollos" who watered? In whose lives have you planted or watered?

6. Which of the following physical stages of life best describes your spiritual stage of development: Newborn? Toddler? Kid? Teenager? Young adult? Middle-aged? Senior citizen?

7. On a scale of 1 (straw) to 10 (gold), how sturdy is your spiritual "building"? How does that compare to one year ago? What are you doing to grow as a Christian? What do you need to do?

CARING TIME
(Choose 1 or 2 of these questions before closing in prayer. Be sure to pray for the empty chair.)

1. Does the group have a person for every position on the team roster (review page M5 in the center section)?

2. What do you look forward to the most when you come to these meetings?

3. How can the group support you in prayer this week?

> [22] **whether Paul or Apollos or Cephas[c] or the world or life or death or the present or the future—all are yours, [23] and you are of Christ, and Christ is of God.**

[a]19 Job 5:13   [b]20 Psalm 94:11   [c]22 That is, Peter

Notes—1 Corinthians 3:1–23

Summary. Paul returns to the question of factions in the Corinthian church. The problem is that by misunderstanding the nature of wisdom (by viewing the Gospel as if it were just another philosophical system) and then exalting certain teachers into leaders of rival factions each with its own "philosophy," they betray their immaturity as Christians. Instead, the Corinthian Christians need to understand that they are God's field and God's building; and that Paul, Apollos and the others are mere servants who assist God in bringing about their growth and their molding into "God's Temple" (v. 16). By pretending to be "wise" (by the standards of the world), they show themselves to be "foolish" (in the eyes of God). They must stop exalting men, put an end to their divisions, and rest in the fact that "all things" are already theirs.

3:1 *Brothers.* Despite his criticism they are still part of the same family. The issue is not whether they are true Christians or not, but whether they are mature or immature in their faith.

spiritual. A mature Christian whose life is dominated by the indwelling Spirit.

worldly. Those Christians who are molded more by the spirit of the age than by the Spirit of God; those whose life and thoughts are so immature that they are "mere infants."

3:2 *I gave you milk.* Paul continues his metaphor. When he was in Corinth, they were not yet ready for "solid food."

still not ready. To his disappointment, they are still immature.

3:3 Jealousy and quarreling are clear indications that their lives are not controlled by the Spirit and that they are still "infants."

mere men. Their lifestyle is not in accord with that of the mature Christian. By exalting certain teachers, they betray their lack of understanding of the Gospel. Paul's point is that although they have the Spirit, they are acting precisely like people without the Spirit. In fact, given the emphasis in chapters 12–14, they thought rather highly of their own spirituality!

3:5 *servants.* Paul and Apollos are not to be exalted. They are merely servants and not of very high order. This same word is used to describe a waiter. They were just carrying out the task God had called them to.

3:6 *I planted.* Paul was the first to preach in Corinth.

Apollos watered. Apollos continued Paul's work by helping to build up a new church.

God made it grow. Their labors alone would not have been enough. The divine life-force necessary to produce growth came from God.

3:8 *have one purpose.* Paul and Apollos were colleagues, not rivals. They had the same ultimate purpose, even though they had different specific tasks to fulfill (one began the work, the other nurtured it).

3:9 *God's field.* The Corinthians are the field which God is plowing via his servants.

God's building. Paul's metaphor shifts from agriculture to architecture.

3:10–17 Paul now develops his new metaphor of the church as a structure which God is building. Note that as in the previous metaphor, this one refers to the church as a whole and not to believers as individuals.

3:10 I laid a foundation. By preaching Christ, who is the foundation (v. 11), Paul was the one who began the work in Corinth (v. 6).

expert. Literally, "wise." Paul continues to develop the idea of wisdom.

builder. (In Greek, *architekton*.) The one who plans and supervises the construction of a building, not the one who does the actual labor.

3:11 A community might be built on another foundation, but it would not be the church. The church's only foundation is Jesus Christ (see 1:18–25).

3:12 Paul describes some of the ways a person can go astray in building on the foundation—namely by using inferior or inadequate materials.

gold, silver, costly stones. These materials will survive the test of fire.

wood, hay or straw. These will burn up.

3:13 the Day. On the Day of Judgment the quality of labor will be revealed.

revealed with fire. The idea is not of fire as punishment, but as a means of testing—a way of revealing the "quality of each man's work." This is a strong warning to those who lead the church.

3:16 temple. Paul tells them what kind of building they as a community are becoming (the reference is not to individual believers' bodies as the temple of the Spirit; that comes in 6:19). This would be a particularly vivid and exciting image for the Corinthians, surrounded as they were by pagan temples, because Paul shows them that within their community—wherever it gathered—God's Spirit was at work creating a new people.

3:17 destroy. The idea has shifted from losing one's pay for having used inferior building materials (vv.

12–15) to being punished for destroying the church. If the Corinthians continue to quarrel, instead of accepting the leadership of God's Spirit, they defile God's holy temple and will be marked for destruction.

> The simple fact is that God's wisdom and the wisdom of the world are at opposite poles. From God's perspective, what the world calls "wisdom" is really "foolishness."

3:18 Do not deceive yourselves. "Self-deception is the common fate of those who mistakenly fancy themselves wise; deluded in this, they are deluded in many other matters. ... They estimate wisdom by the wrong standards" (Barrett).

become a "fool." Should people deem themselves "wise" in terms of prevailing standards (i.e., "the wisdom of this world"), it is not possible for them to become "wise" in God's ways without first turning from the old wisdom (repenting) and then opening themselves up to the Holy Spirit, who brings the new (spiritual) wisdom.

3:19 The simple fact is that God's wisdom and the wisdom of the world are at opposite poles. From God's perspective, what the world calls "wisdom" is really "foolishness."

3:20 thoughts. This quote from Psalm 94:11 refers to plans and philosophies developed by people who ignore God and his ways.

3:21 So then, no more boasting about men! In the light of this, Paul calls upon them to bring to an end their divisions.

All things are yours. Paul wants the Corinthians to remember that leaders and people are all servants of Christ, destined to be sovereign over all creation. It is not that Christians control the world, life, death, the present and the future (v. 22) in a manipulative sense. The point is that these things no longer have final power over them (Rom. 8:38–39). Ultimately, since they are Christ's and Christ is of God (v. 23), the church will triumph over what once dominated it. In the face of such an amazing truth, it is absurd to continue their petty divisions!

5 Apostles of Christ—1 Cor. 4:1–21

THREE-PART AGENDA

ICE-BREAKER	BIBLE STUDY	CARING TIME
15 Minutes	30 Minutes	15–45 Minutes

> **LEADER:** Remember to choose an appropriate ice-breaker if you have a new person at the meeting (see page M7 in the center section), and then begin with a prayer. If you have more than nine in your group, divide into subgroups of 4–6 for the Bible Study (see the box about the "Subgrouping" on page 4).

TO BEGIN THE BIBLE STUDY TIME
(Choose 1 or 2)

1. Growing up, if you had the choice of punishment between a spanking or being grounded, what would you choose?

2. Who in your family is the hardest to shop for—the one who already "has everything"?

3. What is the most menial job you ever had? What did you like or dislike about it?

READ SCRIPTURE & DISCUSS
(If you don't have time for all the questions in this section, conclude the Bible Study [30 min.] by answering question #7.)

1. Who in your life, by way of their example, challenges you to live a better life?

2. What problem in the church at Corinth does Paul address in this passage?

3. How does knowing God will "bring to light what is hidden ... and will expose the motives of men's hearts" (v. 5) make you feel?

Apostles of Christ

4 *So then, men ought to regard us as servants of Christ and as those entrusted with the secret things of God. [2]Now it is required that those who have been given a trust must prove faithful. [3]I care very little if I am judged by you or by any human court; indeed, I do not even judge myself. [4]My conscience is clear, but that does not make me innocent. It is the Lord who judges me. [5]Therefore judge nothing before the appointed time; wait till the Lord comes. He will bring to light what is hidden in darkness and will expose the motives of men's hearts. At that time each will receive his praise from God.*

[6]Now, brothers, I have applied these things to myself and Apollos for your benefit, so that you may learn from us the meaning of the saying, "Do not go beyond what is written." Then you will not take pride in one man over against another. [7]For who makes you different from anyone else? What do you have that you did not receive? And if you did receive it, why do you boast as though you did not?

[8]Already you have all you want! Already you have become rich! You have become kings—and that without us! How I wish that you really had become kings so that we might be kings with you! [9]For it seems to me that God has put us apostles on display at the end of the procession, like men condemned to die in the arena. We have been made a spectacle to the whole universe, to angels as well as to men. [10]We are fools for Christ, but you are so wise in Christ! We are weak, but you are strong! You are honored, we are dishonored! [11]To this very hour we go hungry and thirsty, we are in rags, we are brutally treated, we are homeless. [12]We work hard with our own hands. When we are cursed, we bless; when we are persecuted, we endure it; [13]when we are slandered, we answer kindly. Up to this moment we have become the scum of the earth, the refuse of the world.

[14]I am not writing this to shame you, but to warn you, as my dear children. [15]Even though you have ten thousand guardians in Christ, you do not have many fathers, for in Christ Jesus I became your father through the gospel. [16]Therefore I urge you to imitate me. [17]For this reason I am sending to you Timothy, my son whom I love, who is faithful in the Lord. He will remind you of my way of life in Christ

4. In light of what Paul has previously said (1 Cor. 1:18–2:5), what is significant about Paul's use of the words "fools" and "weak" (v. 10) to describe himself and others?

5. What contrasts does Paul draw between himself and the Corinthians in verses 8–13? What point is he making?

6. What is your reaction to the statement, "the kingdom of God is not a matter of talk but of power"?

7. Reflecting honestly on verse 20, do you feel your Christian life is more a matter of talk or more of power? What can you do to "walk the talk" this week?

CARING TIME

(Choose 1 or 2 of these questions before closing in prayer. Be sure to pray for the empty chair.)

1. How are you doing on inviting people from your "prospect list" to this group?

2. Share with the group a challenge you are facing this coming week.

3. How can the group remember you in prayer this week?

Jesus, which agrees with what I teach everywhere in every church.

¹⁸Some of you have become arrogant, as if I were not coming to you. ¹⁹But I will come to you very soon, if the Lord is willing, and then I will find out not only how these arrogant people are talking, but what power they have. ²⁰For the kingdom of God is not a matter of talk but of power. ²¹What do you prefer? Shall I come to you with a whip, or in love and with a gentle spirit?

Notes—1 Corinthians 4:1–21

Summary. Paul must reassert his authority as an apostle over the church (so he can deal with the problems there). He must do so without negating what he has said about the value of the work of other leaders like Apollos. In chapter 4, he will assert his special authority by reminding them of the role he played in their spiritual life. He is their spiritual father.

4:1 *So then.* Paul draws his conclusions from what he has just taught.

men ought to regard us. His topic is how Christians should relate to their ministers.

servants of Christ. First and foremost, a minister is a servant of Christ—under Christ's authority, doing the work given him or her by Christ.

those entrusted. Literally, stewards. In a Greek household this was the slave who administered all the affairs of the family; i.e., he directed the staff, saw to securing supplies, and, in effect, ran the whole household for his master.

secret things of God. As in 2:7, these are the plans of God once known only to himself but now revealed to all. It is the minister's task to make known these mysteries.

4:2 *faithful.* The key requirement for a steward is that he is reliable in looking after his master's affairs. But the question is: Who will decide if the steward has been faithful? Paul answers this in verse 4.

4:3–4 In fact, neither the Corinthians nor Paul himself is fit to judge his faithfulness as a steward of God. God is the only judge of that, and Paul is content to rest in that knowledge and not let the criticism bother him.

4:3 *judged by you.* As becomes evident, especially in 2 Corinthians, the Corinthians were very critical of Paul.

I do not even judge myself. " 'A good conscience is the invention of the devil.' Paul has one, but sets no store by it" (Barrett).

4:4 *innocent.* Paul has no secret guilt, but this is not a sign of innocence as much as of ignorance. Justification comes not because of innocence (no one is without sin), but by grace as a result of Christ's atoning death.

4:5 *till the Lord comes.* At the second coming of Christ, the Day of Judgment will occur. Paul cautions about making premature judgments. Let the Lord judge. He is the only one able to do it properly, since he alone can see not only a person's actions but a person's motives.

motives. Not just actions but one's personal intentions will be made plain when Christ returns.

4:6 *will not take pride in one man.* Paul and Apollos are colleagues—servants of the same Christ. It is silly to set one against the other. To do this clearly is a matter of pride.

4:7 The antidote to pride is the recognition that all one has was received as a gift. Whatever spiritual gifts they might possess have come from God.

4:8–10 Paul shifts to irony, perhaps parodying what was actually being said, in all seriousness, in Corinth.

4:8 *Already.* The Corinthians are acting as if the new age had already arrived—that they had come into the fullness of God, into their inheritance as children of God, and into the kingdom of God itself.

that we might be kings with you. Paul wishes they were right because, in fact, his present experience was quite grim (vv. 11–12; 2 Cor. 6:4–10).

4:9 *the arena.* The image is of the triumphal return of a Roman general who parades his trophies before the people. At the end of the procession marches a band of captives, who will be taken into the arena to fight and die.

4:10 *fools for Christ.* By the standards of the world's wisdom, Paul is indeed foolish. Still, as he has already shown (3:18), this is the pathway to God's wisdom.

you are so wise in Christ. In ironic contrast Paul points out that the Corinthians, in their worldly wisdom, are acting as if they are wise and superior.

We are weak. In fact, in God's economy, weakness is strength. Christ came not as a mighty conquering hero, but to be crucified as a common criminal. In the suffering Savior one finds the model for the Christian life.

4:11–12a The irony drops away and Paul relates what it is really like to be an apostle.

4:12 *We work hard.* As Paul did in Corinth, making tents with Priscilla and Aquila (see Acts 18:3; 20:34).

4:12b–13 The apostles seek to live out the principles in the Sermon on the Mount.

4:13 *the scum of the earth.* The word scum refers to the dirt and filth removed in cleaning; such a task was given to the most worthless people, and so to be called this was a derogatory slur.

4:14–21 Paul ends the section begun in 1:10. Their preference for worldly wisdom has led them to develop "an arrogant attitude in which (perhaps subconsciously) they patronized their missionaries and ministers and attempted to play them off against one another. Paul's answer is in a theology and a way of life rooted in the cross" (Barrett). By means of the metaphor of a father with his children, Paul reasserts his authority over this church and prepares to deal with their aberrant behavior.

4:14 *to shame you.* Indeed, the Corinthians ought to be blushing in acute distress over how far they have departed from Christ's intentions. Still, it is not shame Paul intends.

warn. The word means "to admonish" as a father might do, in hopes that his children will see the error of their ways and change.

4:15 *guardians.* Tutors, Christian leaders who instruct them in the faith (3:6,8,10).

I became your father. Paul led them to faith in Christ.

4:16 *imitate me.* If they need a model of how to live the Christian life, they can look to Paul: a servant eager to do Christ's bidding and a man who walks in the footsteps of a despised, crucified Savior (vv. 11–12).

4:17 *For this reason.* Because Paul wishes them to imitate him and because he himself cannot come yet (though he is planning a trip), he will send Timothy who will model for them the Christian life.

my son. Timothy was a convert of Paul's.

4:20 *kingdom of God.* The reign of God which is already here but not yet in fullness.

not a matter of talk but of power. It is one thing to make loud boasts and claim great wisdom. It is quite another to live out the power of God. They will see that power expressed in Paul's judgment if they do not repent.

6 Expel Immoral Man—1 Cor. 5:1–13

THREE-PART AGENDA

ICE-BREAKER
15 Minutes

BIBLE STUDY
30 Minutes

CARING TIME
15–45 Minutes

 LEADER: *If there's a new person in this session, start with an ice-breaker from the center section (see page M7). As the leader, you may want to choose question #1 in the Caring Time to facilitate the group in handling accountability issues.*

TO BEGIN THE BIBLE STUDY TIME
(Choose 1 or 2)

1. As a kid, what was the biggest trouble you ever got into at school?

2. Looking back, would you say that your parents were too strict, too permissive, or just right?

3. Growing up, what person or group did your parents warn you to stay away from?

READ SCRIPTURE & DISCUSS
(If you don't have time for all the questions in this section, conclude the Bible Study [30 min.] by answering question #7.)

1. When it comes to judging others, do you tend to be too harsh or too lenient?

2. Why does Paul react so strongly about the immoral brother in the Corinthian church? What does he tell them to do?

3. What wrong attitude toward the problem in their church did the Corinthians have?

Expel the Immoral Brother!

5 *It is actually reported that there is sexual immorality among you, and of a kind that does not occur even among pagans: A man has his father's wife. ²And you are proud! Shouldn't you rather have been filled with grief and have put out of your fellowship the man who did this? ³Even though I am not physically present, I am with you in spirit. And I have already passed judgment on the one who did this, just as if I were present. ⁴When you are assembled in the name of our Lord Jesus and I am with you in spirit, and the power of our Lord Jesus is present, ⁵hand this man over to Satan, so that the sinful nature[a] may be destroyed and his spirit saved on the day of the Lord.*

⁶Your boasting is not good. Don't you know that a little yeast works through the whole batch of dough? ⁷Get rid of the old yeast that you may be a new batch without yeast— as you really are. For Christ, our Passover lamb, has been sacrificed. ⁸Therefore let us keep the Festival, not with the old yeast, the yeast of malice and wickedness, but with bread without yeast, the bread of sincerity and truth.

⁹I have written you in my letter not to associate with sexually immoral people— ¹⁰not at all meaning the people of this world who are immoral, or the greedy and swindlers, or idolaters. In that case you would have to leave this world. ¹¹But now I am writing you that you must not associate with anyone who calls himself a brother but is sexually immoral or greedy, an idolater or a slanderer, a drunkard or a swindler. With such a man do not even eat.

¹²What business is it of mine to judge those outside the church? Are you not to judge those inside? ¹³God will judge those outside. "Expel the wicked man from among you."[b]

[a]5 Or *that his body; or that the flesh*   [b]13 Deut. 17:7; 19:19; 21:21; 22:21,24; 24:7

4. How could handing "this man over to Satan" (v. 5) actually be for his good?

5. What standards does Paul give for relating to those outside the church verses those inside the church? Why the difference?

6. What happens when a church is more concerned with judging those outside the church than evaluating their own behavior and motives?

7. Are you more lenient and tolerant of Christians or non-Christians and why? How does your attitude toward others need to be adjusted?

CARING TIME

(Choose 1 or 2 of these questions before closing in prayer. Be sure to pray for the empty chair.)

1. For what would you like this group to help hold you accountable?

2. How is your relationship with God right now: Close? Distant? Improving? Strained? Other?

3. How would you like the group to pray for you this week?

Summary. Paul now tackles the second problem which has been reported to him: incest in the church. One of the members is sexually involved with his father's wife. Paul is concerned not just with this sin itself, but also with the reaction of the Corinthians to it. Instead of grieving over what has happened, they rather arrogantly accept the whole situation and do not discipline the man by putting him out of the church.

5:1 *sexual immorality.* Literally, "fornication." Since Paul does not label this "adultery," the man's father was probably either dead or divorced from his wife. For newly converted pagans, the whole question of the relationship between the sexes was especially troublesome, since the environment out of which they had been converted was notoriously lax when it came to sexual standards.

even among pagans. Incest was also condemned by pagans (as well as by Jews: see Lev. 18:8; 20:11). Both Jew and Gentile were aghast at the idea of a father and a son having sexual relations with the same woman.

has. By this verb Paul indicates that the man in question was not just involved casually with this woman, but was indeed living with her.

his father's wife. The way Paul has phrased this indicates that she was probably not the man's actual mother, but rather his stepmother. Furthermore, she is probably not a Christian, since Paul does not refer to her again. He only recommends discipline for the man (see vv. 12–13).

5:2 *you are proud.* Paul may mean that they are proud *because of* the situation (it demonstrates their tolerance and their freedom—they are so "spiritual" they do not have to worry about "bodily" sins); or he may mean that they are proud *in spite of* such a situation, even though this ought to have burst the bubble of their arrogance.

Shouldn't you rather. Paul points out that what they should have felt was grief. (How could they be proud when such a thing was obviously going on?) And what they should have done was to discipline the offender.

5:3–6 Paul is quite clear about what ought to be done. He orders the church to cut off the man from its fellowship. In Jewish tradition, such action was taken in cases of severe transgressions against marriage. The person was isolated from the community, and thus fully exposed to Satan as the agent of God's judgment. While it was thought that if the person did not repent soon he or she would experience a premature death, Paul's aim is discipline, not destruction.

5:4 *When you are assembled.* Such excommunication is not done by Paul nor by the leaders of the church, but by the whole church, gathered together in the power of Jesus (see Matt. 18:17–18).

5:5 *hand this man over to Satan.* "To be excluded from the sphere in which Christ's work was operative was to be thrust back into that in which Satan still exercised authority. ... This authority, however, was limited. If a man was handed over to Satan it was not that Satan might have his way with him, but with a view to his ultimate salvation. Satan, in fact, was being used as a tool in the intents of Christ and the church" (Barrett).

that the sinful nature may be destroyed. It is not clear what Paul has in mind here, though probably he does not envision the man's death. Instead he hopes that by exclusion from the church, he may see clearly the enormity of his loss and repent of his sin and return (see 1 Tim. 1:20).

> *Since Christians have been set free from sin they must live out this reality in their daily lives.*

his spirit saved on the day of the Lord. "The thought may be that the devil must be given his due, but can claim no more; if he has the flesh, he has no right to the spirit, even of the sinner. The thought may be simply that of 3:15: the man's essential self will be saved with the loss not only of his work but of his flesh" (Barrett).

5:6–8 While Paul's first concern is for the welfare of the erring brother (vv. 4–5), he is also concerned about the welfare of the church. First he uses the image of yeast as a corrupting agent, and then he refers to the (related) idea of the Passover.

5:6 *yeast.* Literally, "leaven." This is a piece of dough kept out from the previous baking and allowed to ferment to cause the next batch of bread to rise. Jews associated fermenting with rotting, and so leaven became a symbol of evil. On the day before the Passover, all the old leaven was tossed out of the house as a symbol of cleansing. During Passover, bread was baked without yeast, symbolizing purity (v. 8).

the whole batch. Just as a small amount of yeast penetrates the whole batch of dough, so too allowing this one member to continue in his sin will corrupt the whole church. As leaven is tossed out prior to Passover, so too this evil must be put out of the church.

5:7 *Get rid of ... that you may be ... as you really are.* Since Christians have been set free from sin they must live out this reality in their daily lives. There is no place for the old, sinful way of life in the church (v. 8).

Passover. This festival celebrated Israel's deliverance from Egypt. Lambs were sacrificed as an offering for sin (Ex. 12:1–36). Christ's death was interpreted in light of the Passover as the final and ultimate sin offering (Heb. 10:10–13). Thus Christians have been freed from sin and so must avoid sin.

5:9–11 Paul makes it quite plain that he is not calling for total withdrawal from the world into an exclusive cult-like existence. On the other hand, he does call for withdrawal from professing Christians who are involved in open sin.

5:9 *I have written.* Paul refers to a previous (and now lost) letter he had written about sexual matters. Apparently they had not understood his intent and ignored its warning.

5:10 Paul makes it plain that he was not calling them to cut off relationships with anyone who violated the sexual standards of the church. The church, thinking this was what he meant, may have ridiculed his teaching as an impossibility for life at Corinth: there was no way they could live there and do that!

5:11 Paul explains that his instruction applied only to members of the church who, like this man, were involved in open sin. If such people will not listen to the warnings of the church, the church must disassociate from them to show that their behavior is unacceptable. He then expands the categories of unacceptable behavior by utilizing a "vice list." These lists, common in both Jewish and Greek ethical writings, illustrated behaviors that violated common standards of moral decency.

idolater. These are people whose ultimate allegiance (despite what they may profess) is to false gods, including things like power or money (see Eph. 5:5).

> *Christ's death was interpreted in light of the Passover as the final and ultimate sin offering. Thus Christians have been freed from sin and so must avoid sin.*

do not even eat. Dining together was an important practice among early Christians (see 10:14–22 and 11:17–34). This is the practical outworking of excommunication. All contact is severed.

5:12–13 The church is responsible for maintaining a high moral standard for those within it. Paul quotes a frequent verse in Deuteronomy (see NIV footnote) as support for his call for discipline. At times drastic measures are necessary to safeguard the church from behaviors that threaten to corrupt it into something other than a community that reflects God's holiness. This was especially true as the new church in Corinth faced pressures from paganism.

5:12 *judge those inside.* The aim of such judgment is not punitive, but redemptive. Paul is calling for discipline, not punishment.

5:13 *God will judge those outside.* It is God's business to judge those outside the church, which he will do on the last day.

7 Lawsuits—1 Cor. 6:1–11

THREE-PART AGENDA

ICE-BREAKER
15 Minutes

BIBLE STUDY
30 Minutes

CARING TIME
15–45 Minutes

> **LEADER: Check page M7 in the center section for a good ice-breaker, particularly if you have a new person at this meeting. Is your group working well together—with everyone "fielding their position" as shown on the team roster on page M5?**

TO BEGIN THE BIBLE STUDY TIME
(Choose 1 or 2)

1. Growing up, how did your parents settle disputes among you and your siblings? How fair were they?

2. When have you been in a courtroom? What was it like?

3. If you were a judge, what kind of judge would you be: A pushover? A hangin' judge? One known for creative sentencing?

READ SCRIPTURE & DISCUSS
(If you don't have time for all the questions in this section, conclude the Bible Study [30 min.] by answering question #7.)

1. When you are wronged, are you more likely to stand up and fight for your rights, just let it go or look to get even?

2. Why is Paul so upset that members of the church in Corinth are taking their disputes to a civil, secular court?

3. According to this passage, how should conflicts among fellow believers be resolved?

Lawsuits Among Believers

6 *If any of you has a dispute with another, dare he take it before the ungodly for judgment instead of before the saints? ²Do you not know that the saints will judge the world? And if you are to judge the world, are you not competent to judge trivial cases? ³Do you not know that we will judge angels? How much more the things of this life! ⁴Therefore, if you have disputes about such matters, appoint as judges even men of little account in the church!ᵃ ⁵I say this to shame you. Is it possible that there is nobody among you wise enough to judge a dispute between believers? ⁶But instead, one brother goes to law against another—and this in front of unbelievers!*

⁷The very fact that you have lawsuits among you means you have been completely defeated already. Why not rather be wronged? Why not rather be cheated? ⁸Instead, you yourselves cheat and do wrong, and you do this to your brothers.

⁹Do you not know that the wicked will not inherit the kingdom of God? Do not be deceived: Neither the sexually immoral nor idolaters nor adulterers nor male prostitutes nor homosexual offenders ¹⁰nor thieves nor the greedy nor drunkards nor slanderers nor swindlers will inherit the kingdom of God. ¹¹And that is what some of you were. But you were washed, you were sanctified, you were justified in the name of the Lord Jesus Christ and by the Spirit of our God.

ᵃ4 Or matters, do you appoint as judges men of little account in the church?

4. How should Christians handle being wronged and cheated? How does this contrast with what the world says to do?

5. From verses 9–11, who won't inherit and who will inherit the kingdom of God and why?

6. What "were you" before meeting Christ? What are you now?

7. In what dispute or wounded relationship do you need to experience the healing touch of God?

CARING TIME

(Choose 1 or 2 of these questions before closing in prayer. Be sure to pray for the empty chair.)

1. How is the group doing with its "team assignments" (review the team roster on page M5)?

2. How are you doing at spending personal time in prayer and Bible study?

3. How can the group pray for you in the coming week?

Notes—1 Corinthians 6:1–11

Summary. Paul's concern in chapter 5 was not just with the particular case he noted. He was even more concerned with the congregation's need to exercise self-discipline. In chapter 6, Paul cites a second example of their failure to deal with internal disorder. The church has not dealt adequately with disputes between members over financial matters. Instead, Christians are suing one another in secular courts. This is wrong, Paul says. The church needs to learn that it must "judge those inside" the church (5:12). Paul says two things in chapter 6 in response to this particular problem. First, Christians—of all people—ought to be able to settle their own disputes (vv. 1–6); and second, in any case they ought not to be at odds with one another (vv. 7–11).

6:1 Both the Jewish community and certain pagan religious groups settled their disputes internally. Of all people, those who are one day destined to judge the world ought to be able to manage their own conflicts without recourse to the secular court.

dare he. The implication is that such action is an affront to God and to the church.

the ungodly. This is not used in a pejorative sense to indicate that Roman judges were unfair. It was at Corinth that Paul experienced for himself the impartiality of Roman justice (Acts 18:12–17). Here this term simply means "non-Christian."

for judgment. The bench from which justice was dispensed was located out in the open in Corinth—in the market place—which is perhaps one reason why Paul was so upset. In hauling a brother or sister into court, a Christian was not simply settling a dispute. He or she was also holding the church itself up to public scrutiny and ridicule. This is another instance in which new Christians brought old patterns of life into the church. The Greeks were notorious for going to court. The law court seemed to be one of their chief amusements.

saints. This can hardly be taken as an assessment of the high moral standards of these church members, since in going to court they are clearly acting in an unacceptable fashion. Here the term simply means "Christians."

6:2 *judge the world.* In some way or another, on the Day of Judgment, Christians will assist in the process of judgment. Paul's point here stands in contrast to 1 Corinthians 5:12 where he emphasizes Christians are not to be judgmental (censorious) toward the non-Christian in the here and now.

trivial. Though the person bringing the suit might not feel it to be so, these matters are quite insignificant, in contrast to the sort of judgment Christians will be involved in on the Last Day (judging the world and angels).

6:3 *judge angels.* There are both good and bad angels, and even though angels are the highest form of created being, Christians will judge them.

> *Of all people, those who are one day destined to judge the world ought to be able to manage their own conflicts without recourse to the secular court.*

6:4 This verse can be understood as a statement, a command, or a question. Since Paul utilizes questions throughout verses 1–7, it is probably best to interpret this as a question as in the NIV footnote. Paul is asking if the people within the church appointed to deal with disputes are held in such low esteem that members choose instead to go to the secular courts.

6:5 *to shame you.* In contrast to 4:14, here Paul uses shame as a way to bring the Corinthians to their senses.

wise enough. If they are really as wise as they claim (this is their point of pride—see 1:18–2:16), then surely they ought to be able to settle internal disputes.

6:7 *defeated already.* The very fact of a lawsuit is a clear sign that love in the church has been replaced by selfishness.

Why not rather be wronged? Paul counsels non-retaliation, as Jesus had taught (Matt. 5:38–42; see also Rom. 12:17–21; 1 Thess. 5:15). Such a stance is only possible because the Christian knows that his or her true life is to be found in the coming age. "He can suffer wrong in the already, precisely because his life is conditioned by the future. That is, he has been set free from the tyranny of selfishness that dominates the present age. He is free to do this because in Christ he has died and has been raised to live in the new age" (Fee).

Why not rather be cheated? An indication that Paul is writing about financial and property cases, as opposed to criminal cases that rightfully ought to be dealt with by the state.

6:8 Paul now turns to the offending persons who started the whole affair by cheating (or wronging somehow) other Christians.

6:9–11 Paul warns the whole church that they must live out in reality what in fact is true of them. They have been transformed, and so they must put behind the "old ways" (like defrauding one another).

6:9 *wicked.* Paul is thinking of those who actively live out a life of evil. He then illustrates what he means by the list that follows, in which he points to typical destructive lifestyles in Corinth and elsewhere in the Greco-Roman world. These were the patterns of life that the Corinthians had to resist and put behind them, though the temptation to bring these into the church was very strong as is seen in chapter 5 and here in chapter 6.

kingdom of God. Paul continues with this idea of living out the ethic of the age to come, referring here to the time when all evil is undone and God reigns visibly.

male prostitutes nor homosexual offenders. The passive and active partners in male homosexual activity. Homosexuality was widespread in the Greco-Roman world; 14 of the first 15 Roman emperors practiced it.

6:10 *thieves.* The typical target of thieves was clothing which they stole form the public bathhouse or the public gymnasium. Homes were also easy to break into.

> *Paul counsels non-retaliation, as Jesus had taught. Such a stance is only possible because the Christian knows that his or her true life is to be found in the coming age.*

6:11 *that is what some of you were.* Paul is not saying that such offenders are beyond redemption. On the contrary, one senses here his wonder and amazement at the fact that God can and does transform lives—even those who practiced such gross evil.

you were washed. This transformation of life begins with the inner cleansing from sin (which later was symbolized by the outward act of baptism).

sanctified. Paul probably is not thinking of the process whereby a Christian grows in grace, since this word precedes justification in the list. Rather, the idea is of having been made a saint, i.e., one of God's own family.

justified. Acquitted from the consequences of sin because Christ took the penalty on himself. "Paul is not saying that the Corinthians have been made good men, perfectly holy and righteous; it is evident from the context that they have a long way to travel along the road of moral virtue. He claims that, gross as their sins have been, they have for Christ's sake been freed from guilt, united to God, and acquitted" (Barrett).

8 Sexual Immorality—1 Cor. 6:12–20

THREE-PART AGENDA

ICE-BREAKER	BIBLE STUDY	CARING TIME
15 Minutes	30 Minutes	15–45 Minutes

> **LEADER: If there's a new person in this session, start with an ice-breaker from the center section (see page M7). Remember to stick closely to the three-part agenda. Allow yourself 60 minutes for Bible Study if you're following the 12-week plan. Encourage your group to continue inviting new people to the study.**

TO BEGIN THE BIBLE STUDY TIME
(Choose 1 or 2)

1. How often do you exercise? What do you do to keep in shape?

2. What is the best thing you've ever done for your health or fitness?

3. Growing up, how did your parents, school or church educate you about sex: Openly? Negatively? Not at all? Other?

READ SCRIPTURE & DISCUSS
(If you don't have time for all the questions in this section, conclude the Bible Study [30 min.] by answering question #7.)

1. What part of your life do you tend to focus on the most: Physical? Mental? Relational? Vocational? Spiritual? Which do you tend to neglect?

2. How would you characterize our culture's view of sexuality?

3. From this passage, what are Paul's arguments against sexual immorality? Which one is most convincing to you?

Sexual Immorality

12"Everything is permissible for me"—but not everything is beneficial. "Everything is permissible for me"—but I will not be mastered by anything. 13"Food for the stomach and the stomach for food"—but God will destroy them both. The body is not meant for sexual immorality, but for the Lord, and the Lord for the body. 14By his power God raised the Lord from the dead, and he will raise us also. 15Do you not know that your bodies are members of Christ himself? Shall I then take the members of Christ and unite them with a prostitute? Never! 16Do you not know that he who unites himself with a prostitute is one with her in body? For it is said, "The two will become one flesh."a 17But he who unites himself with the Lord is one with him in spirit.

18Flee from sexual immorality. All other sins a man commits are outside his body, but he who sins sexually sins against his own body. 19Do you not know that your body is a temple of the Holy Spirit, who is in you, whom you have received from God? You are not your own; 20you were bought at a price. Therefore honor God with your body.

a16 Gen. 2:24

4. What connection is there between the "spiritual" and the "physical"? How does this make sexual sin unique?

5. What does it mean that "your body is a temple of the Holy Spirit" (v. 19)? How well have you been caring for the temple? What repairs need to be made?

6. How do you feel about the statement: "You are not your own; you were brought at a price" (vv. 19b–20)?

7. If you are to "honor God with your body" (v. 20) what do you most need to start doing?

CARING TIME
(Choose 1 or 2 of these questions before closing in prayer. Be sure to pray for the empty chair.)

1. Who is someone you could invite to come to this group next week?

2. How has God been at work in your life this past week?

3. In what specific way can the group pray for you this week?

Summary. Paul now tackles head-on the confusion that exists in the newly formed Corinthian church over the question of sexuality. This is actually Part 2 of that discussion. In 5:1–13 he addressed a specific problem (incest). Here he discusses another problem (prostitution) and by so doing lays down some general (albeit negative) guidelines. In chapter 7 he will discuss the positive side of sexuality when he examines marriage.

6:12–13 These two quotations ("Everything is permissible for me" and "Food for the stomach and the stomach for food") probably were used by the Corinthians to justify consorting with prostitutes. Paul does not deny these principles outright (they may have actually been principles Paul himself taught in reference to the Christian's freedom from Jewish food regulations), but he does rebuke the church for misusing these principles to excuse immoral behavior.

6:12 *"Everything is permissible for me."* This was probably the slogan of a libertarian party at Corinth which felt that since the body was insignificant (in comparison with the "spirit"), it did not really matter what one did. In one sense, this slogan is true. It defines the nature of Christian freedom, and Paul does not disagree with it. He does, however, take issue with how the slogan has come to be used; that is, as an excuse for indulgent and promiscuous behavior. He argues that while everything may be permissible, not everything is good (much less beneficial).

not everything is beneficial / I will not be mastered. The principle of freedom must be shaped by the principle of love. We should ask: (1) Is what I am doing good for myself or others; and (2) What does my activity show about whom or what I honor as Lord? Otherwise, Christian freedom becomes a cover for self-indulgence. God's law is still important as a means of illustrating what love looks like (Rom. 13:9–10).

mastered. To indulge one's appetites in unsuitable ways is to put oneself under the power of that appetite, and to open the possibility of slavery to a harmful habit. So such license is not really Christian liberty because it produces bondage!

6:13 *"Food for the stomach ..."* Here also in this second slogan, the low view of the Gnostics toward

the body asserts itself. Paul does not directly dispute this slogan, either. Christians are not bound by food laws. Diet is a matter of indifference—especially in that it has no impact on one's salvation.

> *The principle of freedom must be shaped by the principle of love. We should ask: (1) Is what I am doing good for myself or others; and (2) What does my activity show about whom or what I honor as Lord? Otherwise, Christian freedom becomes a cover for self-indulgence. God's law is still important as a means of illustrating what love looks like.*

body. The stomach is one thing (it will pass away in the natural course of things), but the body is something else (it will live on). "Body" means for Paul not just bones and tissues, but the whole person. "Sexual intercourse, unlike eating, is an act of the whole person, and therefore participates not in the transience of material members, but in the continuity of the resurrection life" (Barrett). What the Corinthians failed to see was that the body is the means by which one serves the Lord. Therefore, it is to be used to honor God.

not meant for sexual immorality. Paul now qualifies his acceptance of the slogan. It appears, Barrett suggests, that the Corinthians were arguing that in the same way it was permissible for Christians to satisfy their physical appetite without regard to law, so they had the right to satisfy their sexual appetite with the same disregard of law. This Paul emphatically denies.

6:14 *raise us also.* In fact, the body will be resurrected, as was the Lord's body. (His was not a "spiritual" resurrection. Jesus' body was missing from the tomb.) Since our bodies will be resurrected for eternity, they surely should not be used for sexual immorality.

6:15 Prostitutes were often associated with pagan religious ceremonies. Paul's argument, based on the Christian's spiritual union with Christ, implies that this is the nature of the prostitution in view here (the same problem surfaces in 8:1–13 regarding the eating of food used in these temples). Paul quotes Genesis 2:24 to indicate that the sex act implies a spiritual union between the participants. Hence, to have sex with these prostitutes implied a union with their god as well, violating the spiritual bonding the Christian has made with Christ (v. 18).

prostitute. Paul may not have in mind prostitutes in general (they were numerous in a port city like Corinth), but temple prostitutes in particular. The Corinthians may have been arguing for the "right" to engage in sexually oriented religious activities. Since the body of the Christian belongs to the Lord and is for his use, it is inconceivable ("Never!") that it be handed over to a prostitute.

6:16 *Do you not know.* This is no new principle which Paul proposes, as he shows by quoting Genesis 2:24.

unites. "Joined together." In its literal use, this word referred to gluing things together. In its metaphorical sense here, it points to the strong bonding between two people that takes place as a result of intercourse. Intercourse is not merely an inconsequential physical act. In fact, it is akin to the bonding between the believer and the Lord, as Paul shows in verse 17 (where he uses this same word).

one flesh. Such uniting with a prostitute makes the two one flesh. This stands in contrast to the kind of uniting appropriate for holy people, including uniting with the Lord (v. 17).

6:18 *Flee.* The temptation to sexual sin was so overwhelming in Corinth that Paul uses this strong verb by way of command. The sexual impulse is so powerful that it is generally useless to fight it. One must flee from those situations that arouse it wrongly.

sexual immorality. Not unexpectedly (given the nature of life in Corinth), the Corinthians were confused about their sexuality. In chapter 7, it appears

that many felt marriage should be avoided, and certainly sexual intercourse was to be shunned between marriage partners. So here, the position which Paul is arguing against might be that since it was the duty of a husband to keep his wife "pure," he could occasionally find sexual satisfaction with a harlot if necessary (Barrett).

sins against his own body. "My explanation is that Paul does not completely deny that there are other sins which also bring dishonor and disgrace upon our bodies, but that he is simply saying that these other sins do not leave anything like the same filthy stain on our bodies as fornication does" (John Calvin).

Christ has paid the ransom price in order to free Christians from the bondage of sin. Out of sheer gratitude, Christians ought to flee sin. Out of sheer common sense, they should flee sin, lest they fall back into bondage.

6:19 In 3:16, Paul pointed out that the church was the dwelling place of the Holy Spirit. Here he points to the parallel truth: the Holy Spirit also dwells in the individual believer.

6:20 *bought at a price.* The image is of ransoming slaves from their bondage. In the same way, Christ has paid the ransom price in order to free Christians from the bondage of sin. Out of sheer gratitude, Christians ought to flee sin. Out of sheer common sense, they should flee sin, lest they fall back into bondage.

9 Marriage—1 Corinthians 7:1–40

THREE-PART AGENDA

ICE-BREAKER
15 Minutes

BIBLE STUDY
30 Minutes

CARING TIME
15–45 Minutes

> **LEADER: Check page M7 in the center section for a good ice-breaker, particularly if you have a new person at this meeting. In the Caring Time, is everyone sharing and are prayer requests being followed up?**

TO BEGIN THE BIBLE STUDY TIME
(Choose 1 or 2)

1. If married, when is your anniversary? How long have you been married?

2. What is your all-time favorite love story—real or fictional?

3. If married, tell your "love story"—how you met, how you knew this was "the one," and when and where you got married. If single, share what you know about your parents' love story.

READ SCRIPTURE & DISCUSS
(If you don't have time for all the questions in this section, conclude the Bible Study [30 min.] by answering question #8.)

1. What do you consider the most important ingredient in a good marriage?

2. From this passage, what are some of the reasons in favor of marriage? What do verses 3–5 tell you about the role of sex in marriage?

3. How can being married hinder your Christian life? How can it contribute to your Christian life?

Marriage

7 *Now for the matters you wrote about: It is good for a man not to marry.*[a] *²But since there is so much immorality, each man should have his own wife, and each woman her own husband. ³The husband should fulfill his marital duty to his wife, and likewise the wife to her husband. ⁴The wife's body does not belong to her alone but also to her husband. In the same way, the husband's body does not belong to him alone but also to his wife. ⁵Do not deprive each other except by mutual consent and for a time, so that you may devote yourselves to prayer. Then come together again so that Satan will not tempt you because of your lack of self-control. ⁶I say this as a concession, not as a command. ⁷I wish that all men were as I am. But each man has his own gift from God; one has this gift, another has that.*

⁸Now to the unmarried and the widows I say: It is good for them to stay unmarried, as I am. ⁹But if they cannot control themselves, they should marry, for it is better to marry than to burn with passion. ¹⁰To the married I give this command (not I, but the Lord): A wife must not separate from her husband. ¹¹But if she does, she must remain unmarried or else be reconciled to her husband. And a husband must not divorce his wife.

¹²To the rest I say this (I, not the Lord): If any brother has a wife who is not a believer and she is willing to live with him, he must not divorce her. ¹³And if a woman has a husband who is not a believer and he is willing to live with her, she must not divorce him. ¹⁴For the unbelieving husband has been sanctified through his wife, and the unbelieving wife has been sanctified through her believing husband. Otherwise your children would be unclean, but as it is, they are holy.

¹⁵But if the unbeliever leaves, let him do so. A believing man or woman is not bound in such circumstances; God has called us to live in peace. ¹⁶How do you know, wife, whether you will save your husband? Or, how do you know, husband, whether you will save your wife?

¹⁷Nevertheless, each one should retain the place in life that the Lord assigned to him and to which God has called

4. What does Paul say in this passage to those who are single (see vv. 8–9)? If you are single, how can not being married make you free to serve God? How can not being married make it difficult to serve God?

5. Paul teaches in verses 17–24 that Christians should "remain in the situation" God called them to. What is Paul saying to believers?

6. In a nutshell, what does Paul teach in this passage about marriage, divorce and remarriage? How does this compare to the views of our society at large?

7. Whether single or married, who should have first place in your life (v. 35)? How "divided" is your devotion to the Lord?

8. What is the key message for you in this passage?

CARING TIME

(Choose 1 or 2 of these questions before closing in prayer. Be sure to pray for the empty chair.)

1. Rate this past week on a scale of 1 (terrible) to 10 (great). What's the outlook for this week?

him. This is the rule I lay down in all the churches. ¹⁸Was a man already circumcised when he was called? He should not become uncircumcised. Was a man uncircumcised when he was called? He should not be circumcised. ¹⁹Circumcision is nothing and uncircumcision is nothing. Keeping God's commands is what counts. ²⁰Each one should remain in the situation which he was in when God called him. ²¹Were you a slave when you were called? Don't let it trouble you—although if you can gain your freedom, do so. ²²For he who was a slave when he was called by the Lord is the Lord's freedman; similarly, he who was a free man when he was called is Christ's slave. ²³You were bought at a price; do not become slaves of men. ²⁴Brothers, each man, as responsible to God, should remain in the situation God called him to.

²⁵Now about virgins: I have no command from the Lord, but I give a judgment as one who by the Lord's mercy is trustworthy. ²⁶Because of the present crisis, I think that it is good for you to remain as you are. ²⁷Are you married? Do not seek a divorce. Are you unmarried? Do not look for a wife. ²⁸But if you do marry, you have not sinned; and if a virgin marries, she has not sinned. But those who marry will face many troubles in this life, and I want to spare you this.

²⁹What I mean, brothers, is that the time is short. From now on those who have wives should live as if they had none; ³⁰those who mourn, as if they did not; those who are happy, as if they were not; those who buy something, as if it were not theirs to keep; ³¹those who use the things of the world, as if not engrossed in them. For this world in its present form is passing away.

³²I would like you to be free from concern. An unmarried man is concerned about the Lord's affairs—how he can please the Lord. ³³But a married man is concerned about the affairs of this world—how he can please his wife— ³⁴and his interests are divided. An unmarried woman or virgin is concerned about the Lord's affairs: Her aim is to be devoted to the Lord in both body and spirit. But a married woman is concerned about the affairs of this world—how she can please her husband. ³⁵I am saying this for your own good, not to restrict you, but that you may live in a right way in undivided devotion to the Lord.

2. If married, what is something about your spouse for which you are thankful or makes you proud?

3. What prayer needs or praises would you like to share?

³⁶*If anyone thinks he is acting improperly toward the virgin he is engaged to, and if she is getting along in years and he feels he ought to marry, he should do as he wants. He is not sinning. They should get married.* ³⁷*But the man who has settled the matter in his own mind, who is under no compulsion but has control over his own will, and who has made up his mind not to marry the virgin—this man also does the right thing.* ³⁸*So then, he who marries the virgin does right, but he who does not marry her does even better.*

³⁹*A woman is bound to her husband as long as he lives. But if her husband dies, she is free to marry anyone she wishes, but he must belong to the Lord.* ⁴⁰*In my judgment, she is happier if she stays as she is—and I think that I too have the Spirit of God.*

---

a1 Or *"It is good for a man not to have sexual relations with a woman."*

Notes—1 Corinthians 7:1–40

7:1 *you wrote about.* Up to this point Paul has been dealing with matters reported to him, but now he responds to a series of concerns about which the Corinthian Christians have written.

to marry. The phrase is literally, "to touch a woman," and is a common euphemism for sexual intercourse. "Nowhere in the ancient world is this phrase used to mean 'get married' " (Fee).

It is good for a man not to marry. This statement probably ought to be put in quotation marks (as in 6:12–13): "It is good for a man not to have sexual relations with a woman" (as in the NIV footnote). It is quite possibly a slogan that reflects the position of an ascetic group within the Corinthian church which felt that Christian husbands who wanted to be spiritual ought to refrain from sexual intercourse with their wives. Or, Paul may have been responding to a question from the Corinthians along the lines of "Is it bad for a man not to marry?"

7:2 First, Paul says that it is not good for a husband and a wife to abstain from sexual relationship, since this will increase the temptation to commit adultery.

have his own wife / her own husband. The phrase means "to be married," or "to have sexual relations" (Fee).

7:3–4 Paul now gives the reasons for his views: There is to be complete mutuality within marriage in the matter of sexual rights. This statement stands in sharp contrast to the consensus of the first century, which held that it was the husband alone who had sexual rights and the wife simply submitted to him. For Paul, marriage is a partnership.

7:5 Abstinence is allowed under two conditions: both partners agree, and it is for a limited time.

deprive. Literally, "rob." For one partner to opt out of sexual relations under the guise of spirituality is a form of robbery.

45

prayer. The purpose of such abstinence is prayer.

lack of self-control. Paul assumes that a couple would not be married in the first place if they did not feel any sexual desire, and thus they ought to fulfill such desires legitimately, lest they be tempted to adultery.

7:7 were as I am. That is, celibate; though Paul is not advocating celibacy, as much as resistance against inappropriate sexual expression.

gift. Paul states that celibacy is a spiritual gift! It is not a gift that everyone has.

7:8 the unmarried and the widows. The word translated "unmarried" probably refers here to widowers, so that these words are directed to those who are now unmarried due to the loss of a spouse (Fee).

unmarried, as I am. While Paul may always have been a bachelor, it is more likely that he was a widower, since it was quite rare for a rabbi to be unmarried. In fact, marriage was virtually obligatory for a Jewish man.

7:9 cannot control themselves. Abstinence would be a particular problem for those who had once experienced an active married life.

to burn. When one is consumed with desire, that preoccupation makes it difficult to lead a devoted Christian life.

7:10 (not I, but the Lord). Paul is probably referring to statements by Jesus, as in Mark 10:2–12.

A wife. Paul writes (in vv. 10–11) primarily to women, because it was probably they who were advocating sexual abstinence in order to remain "spiritually pure." This may also be the reason why husbands were visiting temple prostitutes, which was the situation addressed in 1 Corinthians 6:12–20 (Fee).

must not separate. Despite his preference for the single life, Paul does not encourage those who are already married to be divorced.

7:11 if she does. While his prohibition against divorce is absolute, Paul recognizes that sometimes divorce does happen among Christian couples.

7:12–14 Paul examines the issue of marriage to a non-Christian spouse. A Christian is not to take the initiative to divorce his or her nonbelieving spouse if that person is content to remain married.

7:12 (I, not the Lord). Paul means that Jesus did not say anything about mixed marriages—and so Paul cannot refer back to a saying of his (as he did in v. 10).

7:14 sanctified. Not in the sense of having effected their salvation. Paul is arguing against the view that within mixed marriages the Christian partner is defiled. The contrary is true. "Mixed marriages are, essentially, Christian marriages" (Barrett).

they are holy. In the Jewish community, children of Jewish parents are considered a part of the covenant, and Paul probably means this here.

7:15 But should the non-Christian partner leave, the prohibition against divorce does not apply.

7:16 Christians who remain in a mixed marriage may have the joy of seeing their spouses converted to Christ.

7:17–24 Paul now gives the general principle (stay as one was when called), repeated three times (vv. 17,20,24), upon which he based his arguments in verses 1–16, and upon which he will also base his arguments in verses 25–40. He illustrates this principle by references to circumcision and to slavery.

7:19 Circumcision is nothing. A Jew would hotly dispute this statement. "This is … what has to be one of the more remarkable statements that Paul ever made. … In this Gentile church it will be readily understood, precisely because circumcision was never an issue for them. It is hard for us to imagine the horror with which a fellow Jew would've responded. For not only did circumcision count, it counted for everything" (Fee).

Keeping God's commands is what counts. "If Paul's fellow Jew would have been scandalized by his former statement, he would have been quite mystified by this one. From his perspective these sentences would be a total *non sequitur*, indeed contradictory. To be circumcised is to keep the commandment of God. But Paul obviously thinks otherwise. … Almost certainly this (phrase) refers to the ethical imperatives of the Christian faith. One's proper response to grace is obedience to the will of God. … Paul simply cannot allow a religious statement like 'circumcision counts for nothing' to be turned into 'obedience to the will of God counts for nothing' " (Fee).

7:21 slave. The reason why it is possible for slaves to remain content with their lot is because, by becoming Christians, they have been freed from the deeper bondage to sin, death and the evil powers—they are free in Christ, despite their social status.

7:25–40 Paul now instructs those who are not married, focusing most of his words on women who have never been married. His view that the single state is preferable becomes very clear. He writes this way because he feels that Christ is about to return. He ends this passage with a word to widows (vv. 39–40).

7:25–31 Paul gives his first reason why the single state is to be preferred: the world in its present form is passing away.

7:25 virgins. Those persons—either male or female—who are without sexual experience. Here, Paul uses the word to refer to women.

I give a judgment. Paul does not have a clear word from the Lord (see note on v. 12) about whether single people ought to marry, but he does offer his own trustworthy opinion, which he feels comes from the Lord (v. 40).

7:26 the present crisis. Paul probably has in mind the Second Coming. Since it was felt that Jesus might come again at any moment, everything must be put aside—including the responsibilities of marriage—in order to work for God's kingdom (see v. 29).

it is good for you to remain as you are. Again (as in 6:12,13; 7:1), Paul appears to be quoting a truism or maxim from Corinth. But here he agrees with their slogan, though not with how they apply it.

7:28 have not sinned. The Corinthians have probably been insisting that unmarried men remain single. While Paul sees the wisdom of this, this is not a command, but simply a bit of good advice which the Christian is free to accept or reject.

many troubles. Paul is probably thinking of the afflictions of the last days (e.g., Mark 13:7ff, especially v. 17), which will only be compounded by marriage.

7:31 this world … is passing away. The institutions of "this age" are passing away, now that Christ has begun the "new age." When his kingdom comes in fullness, marriage will be no more (Mark 12:25).

7:32–35 Paul offers his second reason for preferring singleness: it enables a person to devote more energy to the service of the Lord.

7:34 his interests are divided. The married man is rightly concerned about how to please the Lord, and equally right in his concern to please his wife. This is the problem: how to be fully faithful to both legitimate commitments.

a married woman. The same is true of a married woman: her attention is divided in a way not true of a single woman.

7:35 not to restrict you. Literally, "not to put a halter around your neck," as one would do in order to domesticate an animal.

7:36 the virgin he is engaged to. Now Paul comes to the specific problem in Corinth. The ascetic party is urging engaged couples to forgo marriage. While Paul would agree with this advice, he takes great pains to show that this is not the only view, and that to get married is certainly not sinful.

7:39 he must belong to the Lord. Literally, "only in the Lord." It is also possible to translate this phrase, "remembering that she is a Christian." In any case, Christian widows (or widowers) may remarry, but only in the context of their commitment to Christ.

10 Food Given to Idols—1 Cor. 8:1-13

THREE-PART AGENDA

ICE-BREAKER
15 Minutes

BIBLE STUDY
30 Minutes

CARING TIME
15–45 Minutes

> **LEADER: If there's a new person in this session, start with an ice-breaker from the center section (see page M7). Remember to stick closely to the three-part agenda and the time allowed for each segment. Is your group praying for the empty chair?**

TO BEGIN THE BIBLE STUDY TIME
(Choose 1 or 2)

1. As a child, what food did you refuse to eat? How about now?

2. How would you describe your diet: Well-balanced? Junk food? Vegetarian? Meat and potatoes? Other?

3. Who gets "the prize" in this group for being the most sensitive to others?

READ SCRIPTURE & DISCUSS
(If you don't have time for all the questions in this section, conclude the Bible Study [30 min.] by answering question #7.)

1. What habit have you had that annoyed a family member or coworker? What did you do about it?

2. Why would eating food sacrificed to idols be difficult for some people?

3. What does Paul mean when he refers to the "weak brother" (vv. 7–13)?

Food Sacrificed to Idols

8 Now about food sacrificed to idols: We know that we all possess knowledge.[a] Knowledge puffs up, but love builds up. [2]The man who thinks he knows something does not yet know as he ought to know. [3]But the man who loves God is known by God.

[4]So then, about eating food sacrificed to idols: We know that an idol is nothing at all in the world and that there is no God but one. [5]For even if there are so-called gods, whether in heaven or on earth (as indeed there are many "gods" and many "lords"), [6]yet for us there is but one God, the Father, from whom all things came and for whom we live; and there is but one Lord, Jesus Christ, through whom all things came and through whom we live.

[7]But not everyone knows this. Some people are still so accustomed to idols that when they eat such food they think of it as having been sacrificed to an idol, and since their conscience is weak, it is defiled. [8]But food does not bring us near to God; we are no worse if we do not eat, and no better if we do.

[9]Be careful, however, that the exercise of your freedom does not become a stumbling block to the weak. [10]For if anyone with a weak conscience sees you who have this knowledge eating in an idol's temple, won't he be emboldened to eat what has been sacrificed to idols? [11]So this weak brother, for whom Christ died, is destroyed by your knowledge. [12]When you sin against your brothers in this way and wound their weak conscience, you sin against Christ. [13]Therefore, if what I eat causes my brother to fall into sin, I will never eat meat again, so that I will not cause him to fall.

[a]1 Or "We all possess knowledge," as you say

4. How is it that what is not sin for one believer is sin for another?

5. In your own experience, where is one person's "freedom" another person's "stumbling block": To drink? Entertainment choices? Political involvement? To dance? Other?

6. What approach do you tend to take toward things that may fall into a "gray area"? How far should a Christian go to avoid being a "stumbling block"?

7. What is one thing you can do to show love or to encourage a brother or sister in Christ this week?

CARING TIME

(Choose 1 or 2 of these questions before closing in prayer. Be sure to pray for the empty chair.)

1. How has this group been a help or encouragement to you?

2. How was the weather in your spiritual life this last week: Sunny and warm? Cold? Scattered showers? Other? What's the forecast for this week?

3. What would you like to share with this group for prayer this week?

Notes—1 Corinthians 8:1–13

Summary. Paul begins a rather long and somewhat convoluted section (8:1–11:1) in which he ostensibly addresses the question of the Christian view of food offered to idols, but in so doing is forced to make a strenuous defense of his apostleship, since his views on this subject of food are not at all appreciated by the Corinthians.

8:1 *food sacrificed to idols.* In ancient cities much of the food offered for sale came from the temples, where it had first been offered to an idol. In fact, this was the source of virtually all meat, since only priests were allowed by the Romans to function as butchers. Jews were absolutely forbidden to eat such idol-food, and the question Paul faces here is whether the same prohibition applied to Christians.

we all possess knowledge. Once again (as in 7:1), Paul appears to be quoting from their letter (see the NIV footnote) which argued that eating such food should be all right in view of the knowledge Christians have that there is one one true God. As in previous instances, Paul agrees with the assertion, but then goes on to qualify it sharply.

knowledge. This is insight into how a Christian ought to live.

Knowledge puffs up, but love builds up. While knowledge is useful, the basic aim of the Christian is love. Sometimes knowledge and love are at cross purposes. When people feel "superior" because they have special insights or esoteric knowledge, this attitude may make it hard to reach out in love to other persons.

8:2 Because the Corinthians do not know that the way of love is to be preferred to the way of knowledge, they clearly demonstrate that they do not know as much as they think they do. All human knowledge is partial. Where there is pride and conceit instead of humility and love, true knowledge of the Christian way is lacking.

8:3 Paul makes explicit the connection between love and knowledge. The important thing is to love God. Such love, then, is a clear sign that a person is known by God (which is more important than knowing about God).

8:4 Paul seems to be quoting from their letter, agreeing that idols are not truly gods because there is only one true God (see also 10:19–22). Still, "Paul himself undoubtedly believed in the real existence of demonic beings, and that these beings made use of idolatrous rites; the fact that they had been defeated, and were ultimately to be completely put down, by Christ, did not remove their threat to Christians." (Barrett).

8:5–6 Whatever supernatural beings may exist, the fact remains that Christians know the one true God (he is the Creator) and trust his Son, Jesus (through whom life comes).

8:6 *Lord.* This title, used for Roman emperors, would call attention to Jesus' divine kingship. It is also used frequently in the Greek Old Testament as the name of God.

through whom. In Jesus, the creative and the redemptive work of God is seen.

8:7 *Some people.* In Corinth, there are new believers who are unable to rid themselves of the sense that when they eat sacrificial food, it is in honor of an idol who has real power and existence, and thus they are personally defiled by eating such food.

> *Where there is pride and conceit instead of humility and love, true knowledge of the Christian way is lacking.*

8:8 *food does not bring us near to God.* Again, Paul probably quotes the Corinthians, and again he gives qualified approval. They are right in understanding that the observation of dietary laws has absolutely nothing to do with bringing a person to God, but they are wrong in thinking that violating such laws brings harm to no one.

8:9 Love for others is the limitation placed upon one's freedom in Christ.

stumbling block. If "strong" Christians exercise their right to eat idol-meat at a temple, this may induce "weak" Christians to violate their consciences, to their detriment.

weak. These are people whose faith is still relatively immature or ill-informed. The "strong" need to relate to them with consideration instead of with a sense of superiority (see Rom. 14).

8:10 *eating in an idol's temple.* Paul comes to the real issue. Temples were the "restaurants" of the time. Social life involved invitations to join friends at such and such a temple for a meal held in honor of the god of that temple. Hence, to eat at such a temple implied involvement with that god. At times, these meals ended in cultic prostitution as part of the ceremony. If a Christian with "knowledge" that "an idol is nothing" (v. 4) exercised his or her knowledge by eating at such an occasion, this might induce weaker Christians who are not so informed to compromise or abandon their faith by again falling into idolatry and immorality.

8:12 *sin against Christ.* Instead of proving oneself to be "strong" and "spiritual," a Christian who ignores the concerns of the "weak" has offended the law of love. It is true that idols are not true gods, that food is a matter of indifference to God, and that Christians are free to eat what they like. However, such "knowledge" must be tempered by love for the weaker brother or sister who will be harmed if this knowledge is acted upon injudiciously.

Worldliness
by Paul Little

I got some practical, first-hand experience with this problem at a student conference in New Jersey some years ago. There I met a fellow, a salesman, who literally worshiped baseball before he became a Christian. He would slave away all winter long so that he could be completely free for his god in the summer months. For something like twelve years he hadn't missed a single game in Philadelphia. He knew every batting average since 1910. He slept, ate, drank and breathed baseball. Then he met the Savior and gave up his idol, leaving it at Jesus' feet.

Towards the end of our rugged and somewhat exhausting conference, this fellow overheard me suggest to another staff member, "Say, after the conference let's go over to Connie Mack Stadium and see the Phillies. They're playing the St. Louis Cards." The salesman was staggered. Incredulous,

he stared at me and demanded, "How can you as a Christian go to a baseball game?" Now I've heard a lot of taboos in Christian circles, but this was the first time I'd heard baseball banned! I was flabbergasted and didn't know what to say. When he asked a second time, "How can you and Fred claim to be Christians and then go out to a ball game?" Fred and I started thinking and discussing the situation. As we talked to the salesman we uncovered his problem. Here was a man like the Gentile Christians in Rome, a former idol worshiper. Baseball had been a thing to him; now he assumed that anybody who saw a game (ate meat), however removed from idolatrous intents, was worshiping baseball as an idol. Fred and I canceled our baseball date since our going would have needlessly disturbed our friend at a sensitive stage in his Christian life. But we also talked and counseled with him, and he gradually realized that not all Christians find baseball a problem. ... he also saw that he couldn't legislate for Christians who have no problem with the sport. It heartened us to see him begin to mature in his attitudes.

We have a responsibility for our weak brother. The biblical principle does not allow us to go along our way with a willy-nilly attitude, thinking, "He's wrong, he's naive, he won't agree anyway, so I'll just ignore him." Nor does the biblical principle call us to conform to someone else's conscience apart from our own investigating and soul-searching. Instead, the biblical principle demands that we examine our motives: Am I doing this and not doing that because of love for Jesus Christ and a desire to honor and glorify him? Or is the real reason a less universal one, a reason that won't hold if I move from one social or cultural group to another?

I've found this a very helpful rule of thumb: If there is any doubt about the propriety of some activity, hold off. But if conscience is clear before God and if the thing can be done to his glory, without confusing someone else in the process, do it with pleasure. Rejoice. Be happy about whatever God has given you to enjoy. This is Paul's clear-cut purpose.

Someone, of course, will always misinterpret and abuse his privilege of personal liberty by taking it as license to do whatever he pleases. Such behavior negates everything Paul is saying here. I'm always suspicious of the one who flaunts his different behavior to show how "free" he is. He's missed Paul's tone and intent by a mile.

11 Rights of an Apostle—1 Cor. 9:1–27

THREE-PART AGENDA

ICE-BREAKER
15 Minutes

BIBLE STUDY
30 Minutes

CARING TIME
15–45 Minutes

 LEADER: Have you started working with your group about your mission—for instance, by having them review page M3 in the center section? If you have a new person at the meeting, remember to do an appropriate ice-breaker from the center section.

TO BEGIN THE BIBLE STUDY TIME
(Choose 1 or 2)

1. Who is your favorite athlete? What quality do you admire about them?

2. Growing up, what prize did you win in any kind of competition?

3. What job have you had with the best fringe benefits?

READ SCRIPTURE & DISCUSS
(If you don't have time for all the questions in this section, conclude the Bible Study [30 min.] by answering question #7.)

1. If you could spend tomorrow doing anything you wanted, what would you do?

2. What "rights" as an apostle does Paul say he is entitled to in this passage? Why is he making this argument?

3. If Paul had the right to the things he mentions in verses 3–14, why doesn't he take advantage of these rights?

4. For what reason does Paul so willingly give up his rights?

The Rights of an Apostle

9 *Am I not free? Am I not an apostle? Have I not seen Jesus our Lord? Are you not the result of my work in the Lord? ²Even though I may not be an apostle to others, surely I am to you! For you are the seal of my apostleship in the Lord.*

*³This is my defense to those who sit in judgment on me. ⁴Don't we have the right to food and drink? ⁵Don't we have the right to take a believing wife along with us, as do the other apostles and the Lord's brothers and Cephas*ᵃ*? ⁶Or is it only I and Barnabas who must work for a living?*

*⁷Who serves as a soldier at his own expense? Who plants a vineyard and does not eat of its grapes? Who tends a flock and does not drink of the milk? ⁸Do I say this merely from a human point of view? Doesn't the Law say the same thing? ⁹For it is written in the Law of Moses: "Do not muzzle an ox while it is treading out the grain."*ᵇ *Is it about oxen that God is concerned? ¹⁰Surely he says this for us, doesn't he? Yes, this was written for us, because when the plowman plows and the thresher threshes, they ought to do so in the hope of sharing in the harvest. ¹¹If we have sown spiritual seed among you, is it too much if we reap a material harvest from you? ¹²If others have this right of support from you, shouldn't we have it all the more?*

But we did not use this right. On the contrary, we put up with anything rather than hinder the gospel of Christ. ¹³Don't you know that those who work in the temple get their food from the temple, and those who serve at the altar share in what is offered on the altar? ¹⁴In the same way, the Lord has commanded that those who preach the gospel should receive their living from the gospel.

¹⁵But I have not used any of these rights. And I am not writing this in the hope that you will do such things for me. I would rather die than have anyone deprive me of this boast. ¹⁶Yet when I preach the gospel, I cannot boast, for I am compelled to preach. Woe to me if I do not preach the gospel! ¹⁷If I preach voluntarily, I have a reward; if not voluntarily, I am simply discharging the trust committed to me. ¹⁸What then is my reward? Just this: that in preaching the gospel I may offer it free of charge, and so not make use of my rights in preaching it.

5. How do you feel about giving up your rights? How hard is it for you to sacrifice what's yours?

6. In this passage we see Paul's deep passion for preaching the Gospel. How would you describe your passion for serving God on a scale of 1 (couch potato) to 10 (Olympic gold medalist)?

7. Paul summarizes this passage in verses 24–27 by emphasizing the importance of discipline in the Christian life. What do you need to do as part of your spiritual training in order to "get the prize"?

CARING TIME

(Choose 1 or 2 of these questions before closing in prayer. Be sure to pray for the empty chair.)

1. Where do you feel God may be calling you to step out of your comfort zone and serve him more?

2. It's not too late to have someone new come to this group. Who can you invite for next week?

3. What prayer requests do you have for this week?

*19*Though I am free and belong to no man, I make myself a slave to everyone, to win as many as possible. *20*To the Jews I became like a Jew, to win the Jews. To those under the law I became like one under the law (though I myself am not under the law), so as to win those under the law. *21*To those not having the law I became like one not having the law (though I am not free from God's law but am under Christ's law), so as to win those not having the law. *22*To the weak I became weak, to win the weak. I have become all things to all men so that by all possible means I might save some. *23*I do all this for the sake of the gospel, that I may share in its blessings.

*24*Do you not know that in a race all the runners run, but only one gets the prize? Run in such a way as to get the prize. *25*Everyone who competes in the games goes into strict training. They do it to get a crown that will not last; but we do it to get a crown that will last forever. *26*Therefore I do not run like a man running aimlessly; I do not fight like a man beating the air. *27*No, I beat my body and make it my slave so that after I have preached to others, I myself will not be disqualified for the prize.

[a]5 That is, Peter   [b]9 Deut. 25:4

Notes—1 Corinthians 9:1–27

Summary. In proposing a serious curb on what the Corinthians have come to understand as their Christian liberty, Paul has apparently provoked a storm of opposition, especially from the libertarian party—so much so that they have begun to question his authority to write as he does. They argue in a curious way: "If Paul were really an apostle, he would certainly exercise all the rights and privileges of an apostle. But notice that he doesn't freely eat and drink, he doesn't have a wife like the other apostles, he doesn't even receive a salary from the church. He must not, therefore, be a real apostle, so we don't have to listen to him."

9:1–2 Paul offers two "proofs" that he is an authentic apostle: he has seen the risen Lord and he has planted churches.

9:1 *Am I not free?* In debating style, Paul disputes their accusations by asking a series of rhetorical questions. He is certainly as free as any Christian, but because of his commitment to the way of love he restricts his lifestyle (as he showed in chapter 8).

Have I not seen Jesus our Lord? A person could not become an apostle unless he or she had witnessed firsthand the resurrected Christ (15:7–8; Acts 1:22). This is the first evidence that he is a legitimate apostle (15:3–11; Gal. 1:11–24).

the result of my work. A true apostle will have a fruitful ministry, and therefore the Corinthians are living proof of the authenticity of his ministry.

9:2 Others may not consider Paul an apostle but the Corinthians know better, since the very existence of their church is a visible token (seal) of his apostleship. This is the second proof of his apostleship.

9:3 *defense.* A technical term for the kind of defense found in a law court.

9:4–14 Since he is indeed an authentic apostle, he therefore has all the rights (the key word in these verses) of an apostle.

9:4 *the right to food.* Paul is certainly free to eat idol-food, but he refuses to exercise this right because it would harm the "weaker" Christians in the community.

9:5 *the right to take a believing wife along.* All Christians have the right to a wife (chapter 7). Additionally, apparently both the apostle and his wife were supported by the Christian community they were serving.

apostles. Those individuals who had seen the risen Christ, and who had received a commission from him. Originally the Twelve, but later others were so designated (Acts 14:14; Rom. 16:7).

Cephas. Peter is singled out because he had probably visited Corinth along with his wife.

9:6 While apostles had the right to be supported by the church, Paul and Barnabas did not exercise this right for the reasons given in verses 12ff—even though the Corinthians felt that they ought to have accepted financial support (2 Cor. 11:7–12; 12:12–13).

9:7–14 Here Paul argues strenuously for rights which he has given up (see vv. 15–18)! This question of Paul's support or nonsupport is related to the larger issue of how the philosophers and wandering missionaries in the first-century world were supported. There were four traditional sources: fees for services, support by a rich patron, begging and work (Fee). Paul's means of support came from the latter, which in his case meant tentmaking (4:12).

9:7 *soldier.* It would never occur to a soldier that he would be responsible to provide his own food, shelter, equipment, etc.

vineyard ... flock. Likewise, a farmer eats his produce and a herdsman drinks his milk—even if they happen to be hired hands.

9:8 Paul has just argued in verse 7 by way of analogy to common experiences. Now he argues from Scripture.

9:9 *Do not muzzle an ox.* In Deuteronomy 25:4 God commands that even an ox be allowed to eat the grain it is threshing.

Is it about oxen that God is concerned? While this principle was given to assure that Israelite farmers would treat their animals with care, the rabbis often interpreted passages in a wider way. In this case, an argument from the lesser (the oxen) to the greater (humanity) was used to teach that this principle had implications for how people ought to be treated as well.

9:10 To the workman belongs some reward for his labor.

9:11–12 It is reasonable for Paul, who founded the Corinthian church, to expect some compensation for the work he has invested in them.

9:12 *we did not use this right.* This is the point Paul wants to get across to the Corinthians so that they might follow his example. While he has the right to financial support (vv. 7–12a), he has chosen not to exercise this right because he did not want his rights to get in the way of the clear communication of the Gospel to others.

hinder the gospel. If Paul had accepted financial reward, this might have been misunderstood by potential converts as the major motive for his ministry. He could have been seen as a religious charlatan, seeking only to make a profit from his teachings. Instead, he chose to work as a tentmaker in Corinth despite the fact that this required long hours and hard work.

9:13 Paul provides yet another example of how a worker expects to live off of his or her work. In the temple at Jerusalem, priests and Levites (temple assistants) ate from the sacrifices offered at the temple (Num. 18:20–24; Deut. 18:1–4). It was a widely accepted idea that those who attended to the religious needs and obligations of others were supported by those worshipers.

9:14 Paul must have been aware of the saying of Jesus, that was later written down in Luke 10:7–8, regarding how his messengers had the right to expect support from those they served.

9:15–18 In verses 4–14, Paul has argued strenuously that he has a right to their material support. Here in his conclusion, he turns the tables and insists on the opposite—that they should not support him! Paul's passion to preach the Gospel comes out clearly in this section.

9:15 *this boast.* His "boast" is that he receives no pay as an apostle, and thus there is nothing in his ministry that hinders the Gospel. His second reason for taking no financial support is that this could undercut his boasting—a most surprising argument, given what he has written in 1:29, 3:21 and 4:7—though he is probably using "boast" in a tongue-in-cheek fashion here. "The paradox of his boasting in his apostleship is related to this reality: God has called him and his churches into being; therefore, he may 'boast' in what God does, even through Paul's own weaknesses" (Fee).

9:16 *I cannot boast.* Preaching is of no great credit to Paul. So compelled is he to preach that he cannot do otherwise.

compelled. "The word 'compulsion' here most likely refers to his divine destiny. To preach the gospel of Christ is not something he chose to do, which is quite the point of verse 17; it is something he must do. God had ordained such a destiny for him from birth and had revealed it to him in the event of the Damascus road (Gal. 1:15–16). From that time on, proclaiming Christ to the Gentiles was both his calling and his compulsion. He 'had to' do it because God had so taken hold of him (cf. Phil. 3:12). So much is this so that 'Woe to me if I do not preach the gospel!' " (Fee).

9:17 Paul has just stated that he is "compelled" to preach the Gospel. As such, he cannot take any pay, because pay implies that he volunteered and this is not the case. He has been entrusted with a divine task.

9:19–23 Next, Paul explains his differing behavior when in the company of Jews and Gentiles. He became all things to all people so as to win them to Christ.

9:19 *Though I am free.* In verse 1, this appears to have referred to Paul's freedom from dietary concerns based on religious scruples. While it carries the same meaning here, it also includes the fact that since he refuses financial support from those he teaches, he is "owned" by no one (see 6:20). He is obligated to no system or group.

I make myself a slave. Since Paul is free, he can voluntarily enslave himself to others in order that he may win them to Christ.

9:20–22 Paul is free to restrict his personal behavior for the sake of others. Thus he would not eat idol-meat when he was with Jews, legalists or the weak. The implication is that he could (and probably did) eat idol-meat with Gentiles (though not at pagan temples).

9:20 *I became like a Jew.* Paul was a Jew by birth, but as a result of his conversion he was freed from the Law and its obligations. Yet in order to win other Jews, in certain instances he behaved as if he were back under the Law—though understanding all the time that this was not the means by which he came to know God.

9:21 Likewise, in other instances, he behaves as if he were outside the Law. Yet so as not to leave the Corinthians with the impression that a Christian could do whatever he or she wanted without regard to its morality, he also points to Christ's law (the law of love) to which he is obedient.

though I am ... under Christ's law. Paul's freedom is not license. Christ's law, the law of love (John 15:12; James 2:8), governs all he does. This implies a moral responsibility to be actively engaged in continually serving the concerns and interests of others rather than living simply for one's own self-interests.

9:22 *the weak.* Those with weak consciences (see 8:7–13) who are not yet free from legalism or from the power of paganism. Paul voluntarily abstained from that which offended the weak.

save some. The real issue is salvation, not just persuading people to join the church.

9:24–27 Paul turns to the concept of self-discipline by way of transition to chapter 10. Discipline was exactly what the Corinthians had most need of. To make his point, Paul uses metaphors drawn from Greek games.

9:24 "The weight of his argument is directed simply against the notion that there is an automatic connection between running and winning. There is none. The Christian must not only start but continue in the right way; it is implied that he must put forth all his strength. The process also implies self-disci-

pline—not a strong point with the Corinthians" (Barrett).

9:25 The emphasis is on the self-control that is needed to win in the games.

crown. In the Greek games, the winner received a crown made of pine boughs. The Christian's crown is eternal life.

9:26 A runner in a race cannot simply run in any direction he or she chooses! The runner must stay on the course. No boxer swings wildly at the air, but concentrates on his opponent.

running aimlessly. Such a runner has no fixed goal. Paul's activities (which he has outlined in this chapter) are not without a point. Everything he does is for the sake of the Gospel.

beating the air. In the same way that he pictured pointless running, now he switches to the image of fruitless boxing. "To get in the ring with an opponent and only beat air is as useless—and absurd—as the runner who has no eye for the finish line" (Fee).

9:27 Paul applies the boxing imagery to himself as he wraps up the discussion of "freedom." Just as it is important for him to discipline his bodily urges (for food—8:1–13; for sex—6:12–20), so that he might be faithful to Christ's call, so too the Corinthians must exercise their Christian freedom in light of their responsibility to love. Otherwise, both he and they might be found to be disqualified from God's race, like runners who left the track. Love, not "knowledge" (8:1), is the essential demonstration of true faith.

beat my body. "His point ... is the need for self-restraint, not asceticism (which he thoroughly rejects) or self-flagellation. In his own case, such 'bruising of the body' probably refers to hardships to which he voluntarily subjected himself in preaching to the Corinthians, which included working with his own hands, and which in turn meant suffering the privations expressed in 4:11–13" (Fee).

The real issue is salvation, not just persuading people to join the church.

---

12 Warnings—1 Corinthians 10:1–13

THREE-PART AGENDA

ICE-BREAKER
15 Minutes

BIBLE STUDY
30 Minutes

CARING TIME
15–45 Minutes

LEADER: Check page M7 in the center section for a good ice-breaker, particularly if you have a new person at this meeting. Is your group working well together—with everyone "fielding their position" as shown on the team roster on page M5?

TO BEGIN THE BIBLE STUDY TIME
(Choose 1 or 2)

1. Which dessert is most tempting to you: Ice cream? Chocolate cake? Apple pie? Other?

2. As a kid, what special thing did you have your heart set on—something you couldn't live without?

3. When you were growing up, who gave you a "good talking to" when you needed it?

READ SCRIPTURE & DISCUSS
(If you don't have time for all the questions in this section, conclude the Bible Study [30 min.] by answering question #7.)

1. What kind of spiritual heritage did your "forefathers" leave you? What kind of spiritual heritage would you like to pass on to your kids?

2. In verses 1–5, Paul asserts that the baptism and spiritual food and drink of the Israelites did not guarantee their protection from God's judgment. What Christian activity or experience do you tend to look to as your guarantee from God's corrective involvement in your life?

Warnings From Israel's History

10 *For I do not want you to be ignorant of the fact, brothers, that our forefathers were all under the cloud and that they all passed through the sea. ²They were all baptized into Moses in the cloud and in the sea. ³They all ate the same spiritual food ⁴and drank the same spiritual drink; for they drank from the spiritual rock that accompanied them, and that rock was Christ. ⁵Nevertheless, God was not pleased with most of them; their bodies were scattered over the desert.*

*⁶Now these things occurred as examples*ᵃ *to keep us from setting our hearts on evil things as they did. ⁷Do not be idolaters, as some of them were; as it is written: "The people sat down to eat and drink and got up to indulge in pagan revelry."*ᵇ *⁸We should not commit sexual immorality, as some of them did—and in one day twenty-three thousand of them died. ⁹We should not test the Lord, as some of them did—and were killed by snakes. ¹⁰And do not grumble, as some of them did—and were killed by the destroying angel.*

¹¹These things happened to them as examples and were written down as warnings for us, on whom the fulfillment of the ages has come. ¹²So, if you think you are standing firm, be careful that you don't fall! ¹³No temptation has seized you except what is common to man. And God is faithful; he will not let you be tempted beyond what you can bear. But when you are tempted, he will also provide a way out so that you can stand up under it.

ᵃ6 Or *types;* also in verse 11   ᵇ7 Exodus 32:6

3. How do the four types of sin committed by the Israelites (vv. 7–10) serve as a specific warning to the Corinthians? How do they serve as a warning to Christians today?

4. If you think you've "got it together," what do you become vulnerable to (v. 12)?

5. What are the four things Paul tells us in verse 13 in regard to the temptations we face?

6. How can the statements and promises in verse 13 help you in your struggle against temptation?

7. How have you been tempted this week? How did you respond?

CARING TIME
(Choose 1 or 2 of these questions before closing in prayer. Be sure to pray for the empty chair.)

1. You are over halfway through this study. How are you feeling? In what way have you been challenged?

2. How are you doing as a group? Is everyone "fielding their position" as shown on the team roster (see page M5)?

3. How can the group pray for you?

10:1–13 Paul now returns to his main theme (sacrificial food) from which he digressed in chapter 9 in order to defend his apostleship. He reasserts this theme by expanding on the idea of self-discipline with which he concluded chapter 9 (vv. 24–27). "The Corinthians took an easy view of sacrificial food (a view that was not the same as what Paul understood by Christian freedom) because they did not take idolatry seriously; and they did not take idolatry seriously ... because they believed that the Christian rites of Baptism and the Supper secured them from any possible harm. This was a mistake which Paul, who had just acknowledged (9:27) the peril in which he himself stood, exposed by the use of Old Testament analogies" (Barrett).

10:1 *ignorant.* Though they claimed to have "knowledge" (8:1–2), in fact the Corinthians had really misunderstood the meaning of baptism and Communion.

our forefathers. Though his readers are largely Gentiles, Paul considers them to be the spiritual heirs of Israel.

cloud / sea. Paul reminds them of the Exodus (see Ex. 13:21; 14:19–31), using the engulfing presence of the cloud of God and their passing through the sea as an analogy to baptism.

10:2–4 Paul notes that Israel had experiences which parallel the basic Christian rites: the passage through the Red Sea was analogous to baptism; the manna they ate (see Ex. 16:4,13–18) and the water they drank (Ex. 17:6; Num. 20:6–13) were analogous to the bread and wine in Communion.

10:3–4 *spiritual food / drink.* Not only did these gifts from God nourish their physical bodies, they had an additional spiritual function (in that they were symbols which prefigured Christian Communion, and hence, the benefits of Christ's death).

10:4 *that rock was Christ.* The spiritual benefits for the Israelites derived from this supernaturally provided water accrued from Christ's still-to-come work.

10:5 *Nevertheless.* Even though God had supplied the Israelites with analogous experiences and sacraments to those of the Corinthians, the Israelites still were denied entrance into the Promised Land because of their sin.

10:6–10 "Some Corinthians believed that their participation in the Christian sacraments guaranteed them against any possible loss of future salvation. They commit idolatry (v. 7) and fornication (v. 8), they might tempt God (v. 9) and complain against him (v. 10) with impunity because they had been baptized and received the eucharist. Paul admits to no such ... sacramental efficacy" (Barrett).

10:6 *examples.* In the same way, "If God did not spare them, he will not spare us, for our situation is the same as theirs" (John Calvin).

on evil things as they did. See Numbers 11:4–34.

10:7 *idolaters.* Paul warns against participation in pagan temple worship (also see note on 8:10 in Session 10).

10:8 *sexual immorality.* Paul now explicitly condemns the sexual vice associated with pagan religion (6:12–20).

twenty-three thousand. Paul is referring to the story of the Israelites' fornication with the Moabite women as recorded in Numbers 25:1–9 (the figure there is 24,000). Paul's estimate is either due to a lapse of memory or it is an error in the text which crept in at a later stage when this letter was being copied by a scribe. "Paul rarely quotes scripture with verbatim accuracy; no one did in those days. There was no such thing as a concordance to help find a passage easily; scripture was not written in books because books had not yet been invented but on wieldy rolls" (Barclay).

10:9 *test the Lord.* The Corinthians (as had the Israelites before them) were testing God by these actions—they were seeing how much they could get away with (10:22).

killed by snakes. See Numbers 21:4–9 and Psalm 78:18.

10:10 *grumble.* They were also grumbling against Paul for telling them not to engage in temple feasts and ritual prostitution.

the destroying angel. It is unclear what Paul is referring to here. Certainly there is ample evidence of grumbling (see Num. 14–17), but these passages do not mention an avenging angel, though "the passages mentioned ... were taken by the Rabbis as evidence for the existence of a special destroying angel, and Paul's noun with the definite article, suggests that he shared this belief" (Barrett).

> *Temptation, it seems, is not unusual nor unexpected. Resisting it is not pleasant, but the Christian can do so. There will be a way out for those who seek it.*

10:11 The Corinthians, in their pride and arrogance, were misunderstanding the very foundation of their faith. Trusting the sacraments and not Christ, they were headed for a rude awakening if they failed to heed these warnings.

10:12 Israel felt it was secure (they could point to God's special provisions for them which were prototypes of the Christian sacraments), yet they lapsed into sin and experienced the resultant destruction. So, too, the Corinthians were headed for the same fate, regardless of the sacraments.

10:13 Paul encourages the Corinthians to stand firm by reminding them that when Christians resist sin they do so in the knowledge that they will be able to endure.

temptation. Paul has identified various temptations which Israel faced: the temptation to idolatry, the temptation to commit sexual immorality, the temptation to test God, and the temptation to grumble about where God led them. To be tempted is to be tested. Facing the choice of deserting God's will or doing God's will, the person must either resist or yield. Temptation is not sin. Yielding is. The Corinthians do not have to give in to the strong pull of their pagan past, nor do they have to indulge their appetites without restraint.

a way out. Temptation, it seems, is not unusual nor unexpected. Resisting it is not pleasant, but the Christian can do so. There will be a way out for those who seek it. The Greek word here is *ekbasis* and was used to describe a narrow pass through the mountains.

Comment

The destructive things the Corinthians have gotten involved in are no joking matter. These are not just peripheral activities "about which men of good will might disagree." The Corinthians are treading on very dangerous ground. They are not far from adopting the arrogant confidence that got Israel into so much trouble. Thinking "God is on our side; we are his special people; we can, therefore, do anything we want and he will just wink at it," they found out to their great dismay that they reaped what they had sown. Paul points out that "their bodies were scattered over the desert ... in one day twenty-three thousand of them died ... (they) were killed by snakes ... and were killed by the destroying angel."

We live in an age of easy morality. "Anything goes." We pride ourselves on our "tolerance." But the fact remains—there are those things that are destructive to us as people. Some things really are wrong. There is a lot of gray area out there in which an action may or may not be wrong depending upon the person and the context. But there is also a black area. Sexual immorality over time becomes a way of life; then an obsession; and finally this good gift of God becomes so twisted that it turns back upon us and destroys our very humanness. A callous disregard of other people is like that too. Doing what we want regardless of how it hurts others can also turn into a lifestyle that becomes increasingly self-oriented and which eventually cuts us off from the very people we need to nourish us. Divisiveness is also like that. As "our group" sets itself more firmly over against "your group" we turn more and inward to a small group of like-minded folks; the world around is viewed with hostility and suspicion; and so we become more and more bitter and withdrawn from the very environment that we need in order to grow.

Nobody likes warnings, but this is what this passage is all about. The problems Paul has addressed in 1 Corinthians are real and they will destroy unless these tendencies are nipped in the bud. Paul warns, not because he hates, but because he loves. "God hasn't made you to live like that," he is saying. "Stop before it is too late."

THREE-PART AGENDA

ICE-BREAKER
15 Minutes

BIBLE STUDY
30 Minutes

CARING TIME
15–45 Minutes

> **LEADER:** *Check page M7 in the center section for a good ice-breaker, particularly if you have a new person at this meeting. In the Caring Time, is everyone sharing and are prayer requests being followed up?*

TO BEGIN THE BIBLE STUDY TIME
(Choose 1 or 2)

1. Growing up, on what special occasions did your family celebrate with an elaborate feast?

2. What is the strangest food you have ever eaten?

3. When have you been invited to something and felt awkward or out of place?

READ SCRIPTURE & DISCUSS
(If you don't have time for all the questions in this section, conclude the Bible Study [30 min.] by answering question #7.)

1. What are one or two "idols" you see being "worshiped" today? When do you find yourself attracted to these idols?

2. What is Paul's simple command when it comes to whether or not believers should eat the meals involved with pagan temples (v. 14)?

3. In supporting his call to avoid these meals, Paul appeals to the Lord's Supper. How would you explain to a friend that eating the bread and drinking the cup is a "participation" in Christ's body and blood?

Idol Feasts and the Lord's Supper

14Therefore, my dear friends, flee from idolatry. 15I speak to sensible people; judge for yourselves what I say. 16Is not the cup of thanksgiving for which we give thanks a participation in the blood of Christ? And is not the bread that we break a participation in the body of Christ? 17Because there is one loaf, we, who are many, are one body, for we all partake of the one loaf.

18Consider the people of Israel: Do not those who eat the sacrifices participate in the altar? 19Do I mean then that a sacrifice offered to an idol is anything, or that an idol is anything? 20No, but the sacrifices of pagans are offered to demons, not to God, and I do not want you to be participants with demons. 21You cannot drink the cup of the Lord and the cup of demons too; you cannot have a part in both the Lord's table and the table of demons. 22Are we trying to arouse the Lord's jealousy? Are we stronger than he?

The Believer's Freedom

23"Everything is permissible"—but not everything is beneficial. "Everything is permissible"—but not everything is constructive. 24Nobody should seek his own good, but the good of others.

25Eat anything sold in the meat market without raising questions of conscience, 26for, "The earth is the Lord's, and everything in it."

27If some unbeliever invites you to a meal and you want to go, eat whatever is put before you without raising questions of conscience. 28But if anyone says to you, "This has been offered in sacrifice," then do not eat it, both for the sake of the man who told you and for conscience' sake— 29the other man's conscience, I mean, not yours. For why should my freedom be judged by another's conscience? 30If I take part in the meal with thankfulness, why am I denounced because of something I thank God for?

31So whether you eat or drink or whatever you do, do it all for the glory of God. 32Do not cause anyone to stumble, whether Jews, Greeks or the church of God— 33even as I try to please everybody in every way. For I am not seeking my own good but the good of many, so that they may be saved.

11 *Follow my example, as I follow the example of Christ.*

---

4. Why is eating at a feast where idol-meat is served different than going to a meat market and buying the same meat (see note on v. 19 and first note on v. 20)?

5. In what ways is a Christian free (vv. 23–24)? How do you exercise your freedom in Christ?

6. Verses 27–33 describe what a believer should do in a relationship with an unbeliever. Do you act differently with non-Christians than with Christians? If so, under what circumstances?

7. What can you do this week to help live out verse 31 in your life?

CARING TIME

(Choose 1 or 2 of these questions before closing in prayer. Be sure to pray for the empty chair.)

1. What is something you appreciate about this group or someone in the group?

2. What is one thing this group could do for "the good of others"?

3. How can the group pray for you now and in the coming week?

10:14–22 Paul now directly prohibits attendance at idol feasts, because he understands such sacred meals to involve actual fellowship with the demonic. It is clear from his survey of the history of Israel (10: 1–13) that being one of God's chosen people is no guarantee that one will not fall into idol worship.

10:14 *Therefore.* Paul will now draw the logical conclusions from his survey of Israel's past.

my dear friends. They may chafe at Paul's authority. They may refuse his advice, but still they are all bound together. Paul is not addressing strangers, but the very people he introduced to Christ in the first place.

flee from idolatry. In the same way that he unequivocally forbids fornication (6:18), he forbids Christians from participating in idol worship. While Paul urges Christians to "stand fast" in the face of evil (Eph. 6:10–18), he counsels flight (not a fight) when it comes to "sins of the flesh." The temptations are too strong to resist. The Corinthians are to stay away from the pagan temples.

10:15 Paul appeals to the fact that the Corinthians consider themselves to be wise. It is a matter of common sense (which they must recognize) that worshiping idols is the opposite of worshiping God.

sensible people. This is said with some irony. They may think themselves "sensible," but up to this point, they have not demonstrated it.

10:16 *the cup of thanksgiving.* This was the cup of wine drunk at the conclusion of the meal in a Jewish home over which a blessing was spoken: "Blessed are thou, O Lord, our God, who givest us the fruit of the vine." In the Passover meal this was the third of four cups of wine. During the Last Supper, Jesus made this cup a symbol of his soon-to-be-shed blood, to be drunk therefore in remembrance of him.

participation. The Greek word is *koinonia*, a word that implies fellowship and partnership. To eat a meal with someone implied friendship and agreement with that person. By drinking the wine and eating the bread, Christians show they are responding

to Christ's invitation to enter into friendship and agreement with him.

10:17 Furthermore, sharing together the one loaf is a demonstration of the fact that all Christians are unified in one body. Such unity should express itself in love for one another. This is another argument for not trampling on the sensibilities of one's "weaker brother."

10:18 *eat the sacrifices.* The priests were allowed to eat parts of the sacrificial offerings (Lev. 10: 12–15), as were others in certain instances (1 Sam. 9:10–24).

participate in the altar. Those who offered sacrifices shared in both the physical and the spiritual benefits of the sacrifice. The basic idea is that those who share in an act also share in the meaning and benefits of that act.

> *By drinking the wine and eating the bread, Christians show they are responding to Christ's invitation to enter into friendship and agreement with him.*

10:19 In and of itself, the food offered to an idol is not changed by that act. This is why Paul allows Christians to purchase such meat from the market (v. 25) and to eat it at the home of unbelieving friends (v. 27).

10:20 *but.* Although food is not contaminated by being offered to an idol, when it is eaten at the temple in the context of idol worship it becomes evil, because it demeans God and robs him of worship rightfully his (Rom. 1:22–25). It also brings unwitting "guests" into participation with evil powers.

demons. Paul knew that the stone idol was just a stone, but he also knew that it was the dwelling place of authentic, evil supernatural beings (see Deut. 32:16–17; Ps. 106:36–39).

participants. Or "partners with demons." The danger in eating at a temple is in developing relationships with the demonic.

10:21–22 Paul is unequivocal. To affirm that one

Leadership Training Supplement

YOU ARE HERE

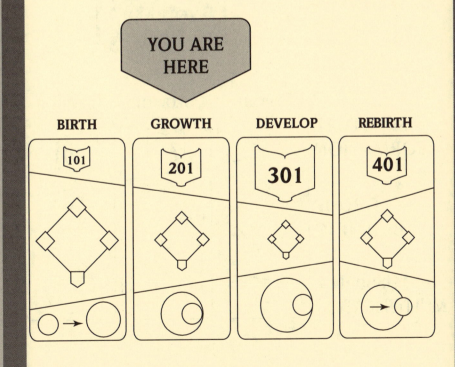

BIRTH	GROWTH	DEVELOP	REBIRTH
101	201	301	401

What is the game plan for your group in the 201 stage?

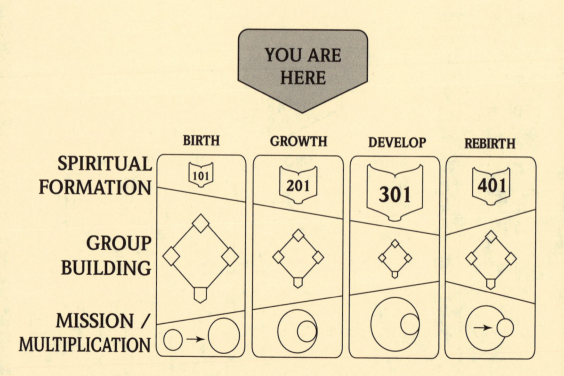

YOU ARE HERE

	BIRTH	GROWTH	DEVELOP	REBIRTH
SPIRITUAL FORMATION	101	201	301	401
GROUP BUILDING				
MISSION / MULTIPLICATION				

The 3-Legged Stool

The three essentials in a healthy small group are Bible Study, Group Building and Mission / Multiplication. You need all three to stay balanced—like a 3-legged stool.
- To focus only on Bible Study will lead to scholasticism.
- To focus only on Group Building will lead to narcissism.
- To focus only on Mission will lead to burnout.

You need a game plan for the life cycle of the group where all of these elements are present in a purpose-driven strategy:

Spiritual Formation (Bible Study)

To dig into Scripture as a group.

Group Bible Study is quite different from individual Bible Study. The guided discussion questions are open-ended. And for those with little Bible background, there are reference notes to bring their knowledge level up so they do not feel intimidated. This helps level the playing field.

Group Building

To transform your group into a mission-driven team.

The nine basic needs of a group will be assigned to nine different people. Everyone has a job to fill, and when everyone is doing their job the group will grow spiritually and numerically. When new people enter the group, there is a selection of ICE-BREAKERS to start off the meeting and let the new people get acquainted.

Mission / Multiplication

To identify the Apprentice / Leader for birthing a new group.

In this stage, you will start dreaming about the possibility of starting a new group down the road. The questions at the close of each session will lead you carefully through the dreaming process—to help you discover an Apprentice / Leader who will eventually be the leader of a new group. This is an exciting challenge! (See page M6 for more about Mission / Multiplication.)

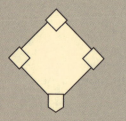

Bible Study

What is unique about Serendipity Group Bible Study?

Bible Study for groups is based on six principles. Principle 1: Level the playing field so that everyone can share—those who know the Bible and those who do not know the Bible. Principle 2: Share your spiritual story and let the people in your group get to know you. Principle 3: Ask open-ended questions that have no right or wrong answers. Principle 4: Use the 3-part agenda. Principle 5: Subdivide into smaller subgroups so that everyone can participate. Principle 6: Affirm One Another—"Thanks for sharing."

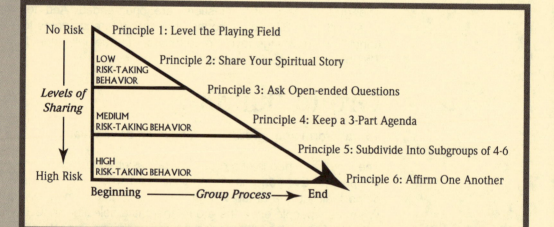

No Risk — Principle 1: Level the Playing Field

LOW RISK-TAKING BEHAVIOR — Principle 2: Share Your Spiritual Story

Levels of Sharing

Principle 3: Ask Open-ended Questions

MEDIUM RISK-TAKING BEHAVIOR — Principle 4: Keep a 3-Part Agenda

Principle 5: Subdivide Into Subgroups of 4-6

High Risk — HIGH RISK-TAKING BEHAVIOR — Principle 6: Affirm One Another

Beginning ——— *Group Process* → End

Group Building

What are the jobs that are needed on your team roster?

In the first or second session of this course, you need to fill out the roster on the next page. Then check every few weeks to see that everyone is "playing their position." If you do not have nine people in your group, you can double up on jobs until new people join your group and are assigned a job. The goal is to field a team. Building a team will better prepare you to rebirth a new group when the group becomes pregnant.

Your Small Group Team Roster

Mission Leader
(Left Field)
Keeps group focused on the mission to invite new people and eventually give birth to a new group. This person needs to be passionate and have a long-term perspective.

_____

Host
(Center Field)
Environmental engineer in charge of meeting location. Always on the lookout for moving to a new meeting location where new people will feel the "home field advantage."

_____

Party Leader
(Right Field)
Designates who is going to bring refreshments. Plans a party every month or so where new people are invited to visit and children are welcome.

_____

Caretaker
(Shortstop)
Takes new members under their wing. Makes sure they get acquainted. Always has an extra book, name tags and a list of group members and phone numbers.

_____

Bible Study Leader
(Second Base)
Takes over in the Bible Study time (30 minutes). Follows the agenda. Keeps the group moving. This person must be very time-conscious.

_____

Group Leader
(Pitcher)
Puts ball in play. Team encourager. Motivator. Sees to it that everyone is involved in the team effort.

_____

Caring Time Leader
(Third Base)
Takes over in the Caring Time. Records prayer requests and follows up on any prayer needs during the week. This person is the "heart" of the group.

_____

Worship Leader
(First Base)
Leads the group in singing and prayer when it is appropriate. Also leads the icebreaker to get acquainted, before the opening prayer.

_____

Apprentice / Leader
(Catcher)
The other half of the battery. Observes the infield. Calls "time" to discuss strategy and regroup. Stays focused.

_____

Mission / Multiplication

Where are you in the 4-stage life cycle of your mission?

You can't sit on a one-legged stool—or even a two-legged stool. It takes all three. The same is true of a small group; you need all three legs. A Bible Study and Care Group will eventually fall if it does not have a mission.

The mission goal is to eventually give birth to a new group. In this 201 course, the goals are: 1) to keep inviting new people to join your group and 2) to discover the Apprentice / Leader and leadership core for starting a new group down the road.

When a new person comes to the group, start off the meeting with one of the ice-breakers on the following pages. These ice-breakers are designed to be fun and easy to share, but they have a very important purpose—that is, to let the new person get acquainted with the group and share their spiritual story with the group, and hear the spiritual stories of those in the group.

YOU ARE HERE

Birth Stage	Growth / Develop Stages	Rebirth Stage
Begin With the Mission to Mulitply	New Leaders Emerge & Subgroups Develop Identity	Releasing the New Cell / Core

Ice-Breakers

I Am Somebody Who ...

Rotate around the group, one person reading the first item, the next person reading the second item, etc. Before answering, let everyone in the group try to GUESS what the answer would be: "Yes" ... "No" ... or "Maybe." After everyone has guessed, explain the answer. Anyone who guessed right gets $10. When every item on the list has been read, the person with the most "money" WINS.

I AM SOMEBODY WHO ...

Y N M
- ❑ ❑ ❑ would go on a blind date
- ❑ ❑ ❑ sings in the shower
- ❑ ❑ ❑ listens to music full blast
- ❑ ❑ ❑ likes to dance
- ❑ ❑ ❑ cries at movies
- ❑ ❑ ❑ stops to smell the flowers
- ❑ ❑ ❑ daydreams a lot
- ❑ ❑ ❑ likes to play practical jokes
- ❑ ❑ ❑ makes a "to do" list
- ❑ ❑ ❑ loves liver
- ❑ ❑ ❑ won't use a portable toilet
- ❑ ❑ ❑ likes thunderstorms
- ❑ ❑ ❑ enjoys romance novels
- ❑ ❑ ❑ loves crossword puzzles
- ❑ ❑ ❑ hates flying
- ❑ ❑ ❑ fixes my own car

Y N M
- ❑ ❑ ❑ would enjoy skydiving
- ❑ ❑ ❑ has a black belt in karate
- ❑ ❑ ❑ watches soap operas
- ❑ ❑ ❑ is afraid of the dark
- ❑ ❑ ❑ goes to bed early
- ❑ ❑ ❑ plays the guitar
- ❑ ❑ ❑ talks to plants
- ❑ ❑ ❑ will ask a stranger for directions
- ❑ ❑ ❑ sleeps until the last second
- ❑ ❑ ❑ likes to travel alone
- ❑ ❑ ❑ reads the financial page
- ❑ ❑ ❑ saves for a rainy day
- ❑ ❑ ❑ lies about my age
- ❑ ❑ ❑ yells at the umpire
- ❑ ❑ ❑ closes my eyes during scary movies

Press Conference

This is a great activity for a new group or when new people are joining an established group. Interview one person with these questions.

1. What is your nickname and how did you get it?

2. Where did you grow up? Where was the "watering hole" in your hometown—where kids got together?

3. What did you do for kicks then? What about now?

4. What was the turning point in your spiritual life?

5. What prompted you to come to this group?

6. What do you want to get out of this group?

Down Memory Lane

Celebrate the childhood memories of the way you were. Choose one or more of the topics listed below and take turns answering the question related to it. If time allows, do another round.

HOME SWEET HOME–What do you remember about your childhood home?

TELEVISION—What was your favorite TV program or radio show?

OLD SCHOOLHOUSE—What were your best and worst subjects in school?

LIBRARY—What did you like to read (and where)?

TELEPHONE—How much time did you spend on the phone each day?

MOVIES—Who was your favorite movie star?

CASH FLOW—What did you do for spending money?

SPORTS—What was your favorite sport or team?

GRANDPA'S HOUSE—Where did your grandparents live? When did you visit them?

POLICE—Did you ever get in trouble with the law?

WEEKENDS—What was the thing to do on Saturday night?

Wallet Scavenger Hunt

With your wallet or purse, use the set of questions below. You get two minutes in silence to go through your possessions and find these items. Then break the silence and "show-and-tell" what you have chosen. For instance, "The thing I have had for the longest time is ... this picture of me when I was a baby."

1. The thing I have had for the LONGEST TIME in my wallet is ...

2. The thing that has SENTIMENTAL VALUE is ...

3. The thing that reminds me of a FUN TIME is ...

4. The most REVEALING thing about me in my wallet is ...

The Grand Total

This is a fun ice-breaker that has additional uses. You can use this ice-breaker to divide your group into two subgroups (odds and evens). You can also calculate who has the highest and lowest totals if you need a fun way to select someone to do a particular task, such as bring refreshments or be first to tell their story.

Fill each box with the correct number and then total your score. When everyone is finished, go around the group and explain how you got your total.

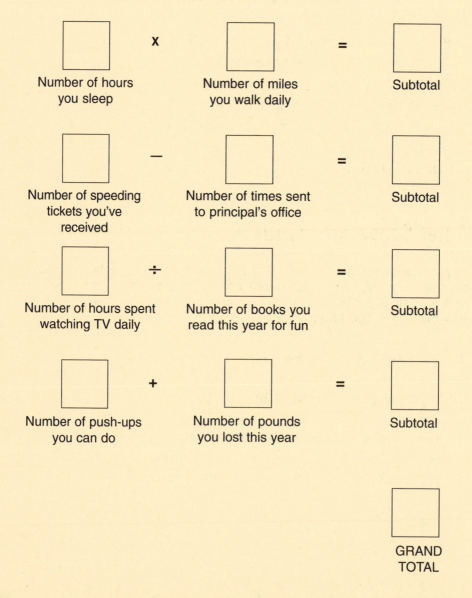

☐ X ☐ = ☐		
Number of hours you sleep	Number of miles you walk daily	Subtotal

☐ — ☐ = ☐		
Number of speeding tickets you've received	Number of times sent to principal's office	Subtotal

☐ ÷ ☐ = ☐		
Number of hours spent watching TV daily	Number of books you read this year for fun	Subtotal

☐ + ☐ = ☐		
Number of push-ups you can do	Number of pounds you lost this year	Subtotal

☐
GRAND TOTAL

Find Yourself in the Picture

In this drawing, which child do you identify with—or which one best portrays you right now? Share with your group which child you would choose and why. You can also use this as an affirmation exercise, by assigning each person in your group to a child in the picture.

Four Facts, One Lie

Everyone in the group should answer the following five questions. One of the five answers should be a lie! The rest of the group members can guess which of your answers is a lie.

1. At age 7, my favorite TV show was ...

2. At age 9, my hero was ...

3. At age 11, I wanted to be a ...

4. At age 13, my favorite music was ...

5. Right now, my favorite pastime is ...

Old-Fashioned Auction

Just like an old-fashioned auction, conduct an out loud auction in your group—starting each item at $50. Everybody starts out with $1,000. Select an auctioneer. This person can also get in on the bidding. Remember, start the bidding on each item at $50. Then, write the winning bid in the left column and the winner's name in the right column. Remember, you only have $1,000 to spend for the whole game. AUCTIONEER: Start off by asking, "Who will give me $50 for a 1965 red MG convertible?" ... and keep going until you have a winner. Keep this auction to 10 minutes.

WINNING BID   WINNER

$_____ 1965 red MG convertible in perfect condition   _____

$_____ Winter vacation in Hawaii for two   _____

$_____ Two Super Bowl tickets on the 50-yard line   _____

$_____ One year of no hassles with my kids / parents   _____

$_____ Holy Land tour hosted by my favorite Christian   _____
                leader

$_____ Season pass to ski resort of my choice   _____

$_____ Two months off to do anything I want, with pay   _____

$_____ Home theater with surround sound   _____

$_____ Breakfast in bed for one year   _____

$_____ Two front-row tickets at the concert of my choice _____

$_____ Two-week Caribbean cruise with my spouse in   _____
                honeymoon suite

$_____ Shopping spree at Saks Fifth Avenue   _____

$_____ Six months of maid service   _____

$_____ All-expense-paid family vacation to Disney World_____

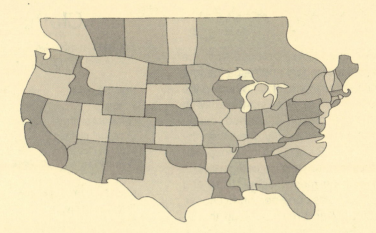

Places in My Life

On the map above, put six dots to indicate these significant places in your journey. Then go around and have each person explain the dots:

- the place where I was born
- the place where I spent most of my life
- the place where I first fell in love
- the place where I went or would like to go on a vacation
- the place where God first became real to me
- the place where I would like to retire

The Four Quaker Questions

This is an old Quaker activity which Serendipity has adapted over the years. Go around the group and share your answers to the questions, everyone answering #1. Then, everyone answers #2, etc. This ice-breaker has been known to take between 30 and 60 minutes for some groups.

1. Where were you living between the ages of 7 and 12, and what were the winters like then?

2. How was your home heated during that time?

3. What was the center of warmth in your life when you were a child? (It could be a place in the house, a time of year, a person, etc.)

4. When did God become a "warm" person to you ... and how did it happen?

KWIZ Show

Like a TV quiz show, someone from the group picks a category and reads the four questions—pausing to let the others in the group guess before revealing the answer. When the first person is finished, everyone adds up the money they won by guessing right. Go around the group and have each person take a category. The person with the most money at the end wins. To begin, ask one person to choose a CATEGORY and read out loud the $1 question. Before answering, let everyone try to GUESS the answer. When everyone has guessed, the person answers the question, and anyone who guessed right puts $1 in the margin, etc. until the first person has read all four questions in the CATEGORY.

Clothes

For $1: I'm more likely to shop at:
❏ Sears ❏ Saks Fifth Avenue

For $2: I feel more comfortable wearing:
❏ formal clothes
❏ casual clothes
❏ sport clothes
❏ grubbies

For $3: In buying clothes, I look for:
❏ fashion / style
❏ price
❏ name brand
❏ quality

For $4: In buying clothes, I usually:
❏ shop all day for a bargain
❏ go to one store, but try on everything
❏ buy the first thing I try on
❏ buy without trying it on

Tastes

For $1: In music, I am closer to:
❏ Bach ❏ Beatles

For $2: In furniture, I prefer:
❏ Early American
❏ French Provincial
❏ Scandinavian—contemporary
❏ Hodgepodge—little of everything

For $3: My favorite choice of reading material is:
❏ science fiction ❏ sports
❏ mystery ❏ romance

For $4: If I had $1,000 to splurge, I would buy:
❏ one original painting
❏ two numbered prints
❏ three reproductions and an easy chair
❏ four cheap imitations, an easy chair and a color TV

Travel

For $1: For travel, I prefer:
❏ excitement ❏ enrichment

For $2: On a vacation, my lifestyle is:
❏ go-go all the time
❏ slow and easy
❏ party every night and sleep in

For $3: In packing for a trip, I include:
❏ toothbrush and change of underwear
❏ light bag and good book
❏ small suitcase and nice outfit
❏ all but the kitchen sink

For $4: If I had money to blow, I would choose:
❏ one glorious night in a luxury hotel
❏ a weekend in a nice hotel
❏ a full week in a cheap motel
❏ two weeks camping in the boondocks

Habits

For $1: I am more likely to squeeze the toothpaste:
❏ in the middle ❏ from the end

For $2: If I am lost, I will probably:
❏ stop and ask directions
❏ check the map
❏ find the way by driving around

For $3: I read the newspaper starting with the:
❏ front page
❏ funnies
❏ sports
❏ entertainment section

For $4: When I get ready for bed, I put my clothes:
❏ on a hanger in the closet
❏ folded neatly over a chair
❏ into a hamper or clothes basket
❏ on the floor

Food

For $1: I prefer to eat at a:
❏ fast-food restaurant
❏ fancy restaurant

For $2: On the menu, I look for something:
❏ familiar
❏ different
❏ way-out

For $3: When eating chicken, my preference is a:
❏ drumstick
❏ wing
❏ breast
❏ gizzard

For $4: I draw the line when it comes to eating:
❏ frog legs
❏ snails
❏ raw oysters
❏ Rocky Mountain oysters

Shows

For $1: I am more likely to:
❏ go see a first-run movie
❏ rent a video at home

For $2: On TV, my first choice is:
❏ news
❏ sports
❏ sitcoms

For $3: If a show gets too scary, I will usually:
❏ go to the restroom
❏ close my eyes
❏ clutch a friend
❏ love it

For $4: In movies, I prefer:
❏ romantic comedies
❏ serious drama
❏ action films
❏ Disney animation

Work

For $1: I prefer to work at a job that is:
❏ too big to handle
❏ too small to be challenging

For $2: The job I find most unpleasant to do is:
❏ cleaning the house
❏ working in the yard
❏ balancing the checkbook

For $3: In choosing a job, I look for:
❏ salary
❏ security
❏ fulfillment
❏ working conditions

For $4: If I had to choose between these jobs, I would choose:
❏ pickle inspector at processing plant
❏ complaint officer at department store
❏ bedpan changer at hospital
❏ personnel manager in charge of firing

Let Me Tell You About My Day

What was your day like today? Use one of the characters below to help you describe your day to the group. Feel free to elaborate.

GREEK TRAGEDY
It was classic, not a dry eye in the house.

EPISODE OF THREE STOOGES
I was Larry, trapped between Curly and Moe.

SOAP OPERA
I didn't think these things could happen, until it happened to me.

ACTION ADVENTURE
When I rode onto the scene, everybody noticed.

LATE NIGHT NEWS
It might as well have been broadcast over the airwaves.

BIBLE EPIC
Cecil B. DeMille couldn't have done it any better.

BORING LECTURE
The biggest challenge of the day was staying awake.

FIREWORKS DISPLAY
It was spectacular.

PROFESSIONAL WRESTLING MATCH
I feel as if Hulk Hogan's been coming after me.

Music in My Life

Put an *"X"* on the first line below—somewhere between the two extremes—to indicate how you are feeling right now. Share your answers, and then repeat this process down the list. If you feel comfortable, briefly explain your response.

IN MY PERSONAL LIFE, I'M FEELING LIKE ...
Blues in the Night_____ **Feeling Groovy**

IN MY FAMILY LIFE, I'M FEELING LIKE ...
Stormy Weather _____ **The Sound of Music**

IN MY EMOTIONAL LIFE, I'M FEELING LIKE ...
The Feeling Is Gone _____ **On Eagle's Wings**

IN MY WORK, SCHOOL OR CAREER, I'M FEELING LIKE ...
Take This Job and Shove It _____ **The Future's So Bright I Gotta Wear Shades**

IN MY SPIRITUAL LIFE, I'M FEELING LIKE ...
Sounds of Silence _____ **Hallelujah Chorus**

My Childhood Table

Try to recall the table where you ate most of your meals as a child, and the people who sat around that table. Use the questions below to describe these significant relationships, and how they helped to shape the person you are today.

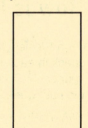

1. What was the shape of the table?
2. Where did you sit?
3. Who else was at the table?
4. If you had to describe each person with a color, what would be the color of (for instance):
   - ❏ Your father? (e.g., dark blue, because he was conservative like IBM)
   - ❏ Your mother? (e.g., light green, because she reminded me of springtime)
5. If you had to describe the atmosphere at the table with a color, what would you choose? (e.g., bright orange, because it was warm and light)
6. Who was the person at the table who praised you and made you feel special?
7. Who provided the spiritual leadership in your home?

Home Improvement

Take inventory of your own life. Bob Munger, in his booklet *My Heart—Christ's Home*, describes the areas of a person's life as the rooms of a house. Give yourself a grade on each room as follows, then share with the others your best and worst grade.

❒ A = excellent   ❒ C = passing, needs a little dusting
❒ B = good   ❒ D = passing, but needs a lot of improvement

LIBRARY: This room is in your mind—what you allow to go into it and come out of it. It is the "control room" of the entire house.

DINING ROOM: Appetites, desires; those things your mind and spirit feed on for nourishment.

DRAWING ROOM: This is where you draw close to God—seeking time with him daily, not just in times of distress or need.

WORKSHOP: This room is where your gifts, talents and skills are put to work for God—by the power of the Spirit.

RUMPUS ROOM: The social area of your life; the things you do to amuse yourself and others.

HALL CLOSET: The one secret place that no one knows about, but is a real stumbling block in your walk in the Spirit.

How Is It With Your Soul?

John Wesley, the founder of the Methodist Church, asked his "class meetings" to check in each week at their small group meeting with this question: "How is it with your soul?" To answer this question, choose one of these four allegories to explain the past week in your life:

WEATHER: For example: "This week has been mostly cloudy, with some thunderstorms at midweek. Right now, the weather is a little brighter ..."

MUSIC: For example: "This past week has been like heavy rock music—almost too loud. The sound seems to reverberate off the walls."

COLOR: For example: "This past week has been mostly fall colors—deep orange, flaming red and pumpkin."

SEASON OF THE YEAR: For example: "This past week has been like springtime. New signs of life are beginning to appear on the barren trees, and a few shoots of winter wheat are breaking through the frozen ground."

My Spiritual Journey

The half-finished sentences below are designed to help you share your spiritual story. Ask one person to finish all the sentences. Then move to the next person, etc. If you are short on time, have only one person tell their story in this session.

1. RELIGIOUS BACKGROUND: My spiritual story begins in my home as a child, where the religious training was ...

2. CHURCH: The church that I went to as a child was ...

3. SIGNIFICANT PERSON: The person who had the greatest influence on my spiritual formation was ...

4. PERSONAL ENCOUNTER: The first time God became more than just a name to me was when ...

5. JOURNEY: Since my personal encounter with God, my Christian life might be described as ...

6. PRESENT: On a scale from 1 to 10, I would describe my spiritual energy level right now as a ...

7. NEXT STEP: The thing I need to work on right now in my spiritual life is ...

Bragging Rights

Check your group for bragging rights in these categories.

❒ SPEEDING TICKETS: the person with the most speeding tickets
❒ BROKEN BONES: the person with the most broken bones
❒ STITCHES: the person with the most stitches
❒ SCARS: the person with the longest scar
❒ FISH OR GAME: the person who claims they caught the largest fish or killed the largest animal
❒ STUNTS: the person with the most death-defying story
❒ IRON: the person who can pump the most iron

Personal Habits

Have everyone in your group finish the sentence on the first category by putting an "**X**" somewhere between the two extremes (e.g., on HOUSEWORK ... I would put myself closer to "Where's the floor?"). Repeat this process down the list as time permits.

ON HOUSEWORK, I AM SOMEWHERE BETWEEN:
Eat off the floor_____Where's the floor?

ON COOKING, I AM SOMEWHERE BETWEEN:
Every meal is an act of worship_____Make it fast and hold the frills

ON EXERCISING, I AM SOMEWHERE BETWEEN:
Workout every morning_____Click the remote

ON SHOPPING, I AM SOMEWHERE BETWEEN:
Shop all day for a bargain_____Only the best

ON EATING, I AM SOMEWHERE BETWEEN:
You are what you eat_____Eat, drink and be merry

American Graffiti

If Hollywood made a movie about your life on the night of your high school prom, what would be needed? Let each person in your group have a few minutes to recall these details. If you have more than four or five in your group, ask everyone to choose two or three topics to talk about.

1. LOCATION: Where were you living?
2. WEIGHT: How much did you weigh—soaking wet?
3. PROM: Where was it held?
4. DATE: Who did you go with?
5. CAR / TRANSPORTATION: How did you get there?
   (If you used a car, what was the model, year, color, condition?)
6. ATTIRE: What did you wear?
7. PROGRAM: What was the entertainment?
8. AFTERWARD: What did you do afterward?
9. HIGHLIGHT: What was the highlight of the evening?
10. HOMECOMING: If you could go back and visit your high school, who would you like to see?

Group Orchestra

Read out loud the first item and let everyone nominate the person in your group for this musical instrument in your group orchestra. Then, read aloud the next instrument, and call out another name, etc.

ANGELIC HARP: Soft, gentle, melodious, wooing with heavenly sounds.

OLD-FASHIONED WASHBOARD: Nonconforming, childlike and fun.

PLAYER PIANO: Mischievous, raucous, honky-tonk—delightfully carefree.

KETTLEDRUM: Strong, vibrant, commanding when needed but usually in the background.

PASSIONATE CASTANET: Full of Spanish fervor—intense and always upbeat.

STRADIVARIUS VIOLIN: Priceless, exquisite, soul-piercing—with the touch of the master.

FLUTTERING FLUTE: Tender, lighthearted, wide-ranging and clear as crystal.

SCOTTISH BAGPIPES: Forthright, distinctive and unmistakable.

SQUARE DANCE FIDDLE: Folksy, down-to-earth, toe-tapping—sprightly and full of energy.

ENCHANTING OBOE: Haunting, charming, disarming—even the cobra is harmless with this sound.

MELLOW CELLO: Deep, sonorous, compassionate—adding body and depth to the orchestra.

PIPE ORGAN: Grand, magnificent, rich—versatile and commanding.

HERALDING TRUMPET: Stirring, lively, invigorating—signaling attention and attack.

CLASSICAL GUITAR: Contemplative, profound, thoughtful *and* thought-provoking.

ONE-MAN BAND: Able to do many things well, all at once.

COMB AND TISSUE PAPER: Makeshift, original, uncomplicated—homespun and creative.

SWINGING TROMBONE: Warm, rich—great in solo or background support.

Broadway Show

Imagine for a moment that your group has been chosen to produce a Broadway show, and you have to choose people from your group for all of the jobs for this production. Have someone read out loud the job description for the first job below—PRODUCER. Then, let everyone in your group call out the name of the person in your group who would best fit this job. (You don't have to agree.) Then read the job description for the next job and let everyone nominate another person, etc. You only have 10 minutes for this assignment, so move fast.

PRODUCER: Typical Hollywood business tycoon; extravagant, big-budget, big-production magnate in the Steven Spielberg style.

DIRECTOR: Creative, imaginative brains who coordinates the production and draws the best out of others.

HEROINE: Beautiful, captivating, everybody's heart throb; defenseless when men are around, but nobody's fool.

HERO: Tough, macho, champion of the underdog, knight in shining armor; defender of truth.

COMEDIAN: Childlike, happy-go-lucky, outrageously funny, keeps everyone laughing.

CHARACTER PERSON: Rugged individualist, outrageously different, colorful, adds spice to any surrounding.

FALL GUY: Easy-going, nonchalant character who wins the hearts of everyone by being the "foil" of the heavy characters.

TECHNICAL DIRECTOR: The genius for "sound and lights"; creates the perfect atmosphere.

COMPOSER OF LYRICS: Communicates in music what everybody understands; heavy into feelings, moods, outbursts of energy.

PUBLICITY AGENT: Advertising and public relations expert; knows all the angles, good at one-liners, a flair for "hot" news.

VILLAIN: The "bad guy" who really is the heavy for the plot, forces others to think, challenges traditional values; out to destroy anything artificial or hypocritical.

AUTHOR: Shy, aloof; very much in touch with feelings, sensitive to people, puts into words what others only feel.

STAGEHAND: Supportive, behind-the-scenes person who makes things run smoothly; patient and tolerant.

Wild Predictions

Try to match the people in your group to the crazy forecasts below. (Don't take it too seriously; it's meant to be fun!) Read out loud the first item and ask everyone to call out the name of the person who is most likely to accomplish this feat. Then, read the next item and ask everyone to make a new prediction, etc.

THE PERSON IN OUR GROUP MOST LIKELY TO ...

Make a million selling Beanie Babies over the Internet

Become famous for designing new attire for sumo wrestlers

Replace Vanna White on *Wheel of Fortune*

Appear on *The Tonight Show* to exhibit an acrobatic talent

Move to a desert island

Discover a new use for underarm deodorant

Succeed David Letterman as host of *The Late Show*

Substitute for John Madden as Fox's football color analyst

Appear on the cover of *Muscle & Fitness Magazine*

Become the newest member of the Spice Girls

Work as a bodyguard for Rush Limbaugh at Feminist convention

Write a best-selling novel based on their love life

Be a dance instructor on a cruise ship for wealthy, well-endowed widows

Win the blue ribbon at the state fair for best Rocky Mountain oyster recipe

Land a job as head librarian for Amazon.com

Be the first woman to win the Indianapolis 500

Open the Clouseau Private Detective Agency

Career Placements

Read the list of career choices aloud and quickly choose someone in your group for each job—based upon their unique gifts and talents. Have fun!

SPACE ENVIRONMENTAL ENGINEER: in charge of designing the bathrooms on space shuttles

SCHOOL BUS DRIVER: for junior high kids in New York City (earplugs supplied)

WRITER: of an "advice to the lovelorn" column in Hollywood

SUPERVISOR: of a complaint department for a large automobile dealership and service department

ANIMAL PSYCHIATRIST: for French poodles in a fashionable suburb of Paris

RESEARCH SCIENTIST: studying the fertilization patterns of the dodo bird—now extinct

SAFARI GUIDE: in the heart of Africa—for wealthy widows and eccentric bachelors

LITTLE LEAGUE BASEBALL COACH: in Mudville, Illinois—last year's record was 0 and 12

MANAGER: of your local McDonald's during the holiday rush with 210 teenage employees

LIBRARIAN: for the Walt Disney Hall of Fame memorabilia

CHOREOGRAPHER: for the Dallas Cowboys cheerleaders

NURSE'S AIDE: at a home for retired Sumo wrestlers

SECURITY GUARD: crowd control officer at a rock concert

ORGANIZER: of paperwork for Congress

PUBLIC RELATIONS MANAGER: for Dennis Rodman

BODYGUARD: for Rush Limbaugh on a speaking tour of feminist groups

TOY ASSEMBLY PERSON: for a toy store over the holidays

You and Me, Partner

Think of the people in your group as you read over the list of activities below. If you had to choose someone from your group to be your partner, who would you choose to do these activities with? Jot down each person's name beside the activity. You can use each person's name only once and you have to use everyone's name once—so think it through before you jot down their names. Then, let one person listen to what others chose for them. Then, move to the next person, etc., around your group.

WHO WOULD YOU CHOOSE FOR THE FOLLOWING?

_____ ENDURANCE DANCE CONTEST partner

_____ BOBSLED RACE partner for the Olympics

_____ TRAPEZE ACT partner

_____ MY UNDERSTUDY for my debut in a Broadway musical

_____ BEST MAN or MAID OF HONOR at my wedding

_____ SECRET UNDERCOVER AGENT copartner

_____ BODYGUARD for me when I strike it rich

_____ MOUNTAIN CLIMBING partner in climbing Mt. Everest

_____ ASTRONAUT to fly the space shuttle while I walk in space

_____ SAND CASTLE TOURNAMENT building partner

_____ PIT CREW foreman for entry in Indianapolis 500

_____ AUTHOR for my biography

_____ SURGEON to operate on me for a life-threatening cancer

_____ NEW BUSINESS START-UP partner

_____ TAG-TEAM partner for a professional wrestling match

_____ HEAVY-DUTY PRAYER partner

My Gourmet Group

Here's a chance to pass out some much deserved praise for the people who have made your group something special. Ask one person to sit in silence while the others explain the delicacy they would choose to describe the contribution this person has made to your group. Repeat the process for each member of the group.

CAVIAR: That special touch of class and aristocratic taste that has made the rest of us feel like royalty.

PRIME RIB: Stable, brawny, macho, the generous mainstay of any menu; juicy, mouth-watering "perfect cut" for good nourishment.

IMPORTED CHEESE: Distinctive, tangy, mellow with age; adds depth to any meal.

VINEGAR AND OIL: Tart, witty, dry; a rare combination of healing ointment and pungent spice to add "bite" to the salad.

ARTICHOKE HEARTS: Tender and disarmingly vulnerable; whets the appetite for heartfelt sharing.

FRENCH PASTRY: Tempting, irresistible "creme de la creme" dessert; the connoisseur's delight for topping off a meal.

PHEASANT UNDER GLASS: Wild, totally unique, a rare dish for people who appreciate original fare.

CARAFE OF WINE: Sparkling, effervescent, exuberant and joyful; outrageously free and liberating to the rest of us.

ESCARGOT AND OYSTERS: Priceless treasures of the sea once out of their shells; succulent, delicate and irreplaceable.

FRESH FRUIT: Vine-ripened, energy-filled, invigorating; the perfect treat after a heavy meal.

ITALIAN ICE CREAMS: Colorful, flavorful, delightfully childlike; the unexpected surprise in our group.

Thank You

How would you describe your experience with this group? Choose one of the animals below that best describes how your experience in this group affected your life. Then share your responses with the group.

WILD EAGLE: You have helped to heal my wings, and taught me how to soar again.

TOWERING GIRAFFE: You have helped me to hold my head up and stick my neck out, and reach over the fences I have built.

PLAYFUL PORPOISE: You have helped me to find a new freedom and a whole new world to play in.

COLORFUL PEACOCK: You have told me that I'm beautiful; I've started to believe it, and it's changing my life.

SAFARI ELEPHANT: I have enjoyed this new adventure, and I'm not going to forget it, or this group; I can hardly wait for the next safari.

LOVABLE HIPPOPOTAMUS: You have let me surface and bask in the warm sunshine of God's love.

LANKY LEOPARD: You have helped me to look closely at myself and see some spots, and you still accept me the way I am.

DANCING BEAR: You have taught me to dance in the midst of pain, and you have helped me to reach out and hug again.

ALL-WEATHER DUCK: You have helped me to celebrate life—even in stormy weather—and to sing in the rain.

Academy Awards

You have had a chance to observe the gifts and talents of the members of your group. Now you will have a chance to pass out some much deserved praise for the contribution that each member of the group has made to your life. Read out loud the first award. Then let everyone nominate the person they feel is the most deserving for that award. Then read the next award, etc., through the list. Have fun!

SPARK PLUG AWARD: for the person who ignited the group

DEAR ABBY AWARD: for the person who cared enough to listen

ROYAL GIRDLE AWARD: for the person who supported us

WINNIE THE POOH AWARD: for the warm, caring person when someone needed a hug

ROCK OF GIBRALTER AWARD: for the person who was strong in the tough times of our group

OPRAH AWARD: for the person who asked the fun questions that got us to talk

TED KOPPEL AWARD: for the person who asked the heavy questions that made us think

KING ARTHUR'S AWARD: for the knight in shining armor

PINK PANTHER AWARD: for the detective who made us deal with Scripture

NOBEL PEACE PRIZE: for the person who harmonized our differences of opinion without diminishing anyone

BIG MAC AWARD: for the person who showed the biggest hunger for spiritual things

SERENDIPITY CROWN: for the person who grew the most spiritually during the course—in your estimation

You Remind Me of Jesus

Every Christian reflects the character of Jesus in some way. As your group has gotten to know each other, you can begin to see how each person demonstrates Christ in their very own personality. Go around the circle and have each person listen while others take turns telling that person what they notice in him or her that reminds them of Jesus. You may also want to tell them why you selected what you did.

YOU REMIND ME OF ...

JESUS THE HEALER: You seem to be able to touch someone's life with your compassion and help make them whole.

JESUS THE SERVANT: There's nothing that you wouldn't do for someone.

JESUS THE PREACHER: You share your faith in a way that challenges and inspires people.

JESUS THE LEADER: As Jesus had a plan for the disciples, you are able to lead others in a way that honors God.

JESUS THE REBEL: By doing the unexpected, you remind me of Jesus' way of revealing God in unique, surprising ways.

JESUS THE RECONCILER: Like Jesus, you have the ability to be a peacemaker between others.

JESUS THE TEACHER: You have a gift for bringing light and understanding to God's Word.

JESUS THE CRITIC: You have the courage to say what needs to be said, even if it isn't always popular.

JESUS THE SACRIFICE: Like Jesus, you seem willing to sacrifice anything to glorify God.

Reflections

Take some time to evaluate the life of your group by using the statements below. Read the first sentence out loud and ask everyone to explain where they would put a dot between the two extremes. When you are finished, go back and give your group an overall grade in the category of Group Building, Bible Study and Mission.

◇ GROUP BUILDING

On celebrating life and having fun together, we were more like a ...
wet blanket _____ hot tub

On becoming a caring community, we were more like a ...
prickly porcupine _____ cuddly teddy bear

📖 SPIRITUAL FORMATION (Bible Study)

On sharing our spiritual stories, we were more like a ...
shallow pond _____ spring-fed lake

On digging into Scripture, we were more like a ...
slow-moving snail _____ voracious anteater

◯ MISSION

On inviting new people into our group, we were more like a ...
barbed-wire fence _____ wide-open door

On stretching our vision for mission, we were more like an ...
ostrich _____ eagle

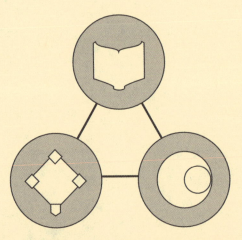

Human Bingo / Party Mixer

After the leader says "Go!" circulate the room, asking people the things described in the boxes. If someone answers "Yes" to a question, have them sign their initials in that box. Continue until someone completes the entire card—or one row if you don't have that much time. You can only use someone's name twice, and you cannot use your own name on your card.

can juggle	TP'd a house	never used an outhouse	sings in the shower	rec'd 6+ traffic tickets	paddled in school	watches Sesame Street
sleeps in church regularly	never changed a diaper	split pants in public	milked a cow	born out of the country	has been to Hawaii	can do the splits
watches soap operas	can touch tongue to nose	rode a motor-cycle	never ridden a horse	moved twice last year	sleeps on a waterbed	has hole in sock
walked in wrong restroom	loves classical music	skipped school	**FREE**	broke a leg	has a hot tub	loves eating sushi
is an only child	loves raw oysters	has a 3-inch + scar	doesn't wear PJ's	smoked a cigar	can dance the Charleston	weighs under 110 lbs.
likes writing poetry	still has tonsils	loves crossword puzzles	likes bubble baths	wearing Fruit of the Loom	doesn't use mouth-wash	often watches cartoons
kissed on first date	can wiggle ears	can play the guitar	plays chess regularly	reads the comics first	can touch palms to floor	sleeps with stuffed animal

Group Covenant

Any group can benefit from creating a group covenant. Reserve some time during one of the first meetings to discuss answers to the following questions. When everyone in the group has the same expectations for the group, everything runs more smoothly.

1. The purpose of our group is:

2. The goals of our group are:

3. We will meet for _____ weeks, after which we will decide if we wish to continue as a group. If we do decide to continue, we will reconsider this covenant.

4. We will meet _____ (weekly, every other week, monthly).

5. Our meetings will be from _____ o'clock to _____ o'clock, and we will strive to start and end on time.

6. We will meet at _____
   or rotate from house to house.

7. We will take care of the following details: ❏ child care ❏ refreshments

8. We agree to the following rules for our group:

   ❏ PRIORITY: While we are in this group, group meetings have priority.

   ❏ PARTICIPATION: Everyone is given the right to their own opinion and all questions are respected.

   ❏ CONFIDENTIALITY: Anything said in the meeting is not to be repeated outside the meeting.

   ❏ EMPTY CHAIR: The group stays open to new people and invites prospective members to visit the group.

   ❏ SUPPORT: Permission is given to call each other in times of need.

   ❏ ADVICE GIVING: Unsolicited advice is not allowed.

   ❏ MISSION: We will do all that is in our power to start a new group.

can participate in both the Lord's Supper and in a demon feast at a temple is to incur the wrath of God who continually warned Israel to forsake idolatry (Ex. 20:3–4; 2 Cor. 6:14–16).

10:23–11:1 Paul now sums up the discussion he began in 8:1 concerning food offered to idols by setting out specific, practical instructions.

10:23 In 6:12 Paul examined the implications of this maxim for an individual Christian, warning that unrestrained personal freedom can lead to a form of bondage. Here, he examines the implications of this maxim for the church as a whole, arguing that "the freedom of the Christian is the freedom to play his part in the upbuilding of the community" (Barth).

10:24 This is the maxim that ought to guide their behavior.

others. Christians ought to seek good, not just for their friends, but also for those who are unlike them. Specifically, Paul is urging consideration for those who disagree about eating idol-food.

10:25 It does not matter what one eats—food offered to idols or food prohibited by strict Jewish dietary laws. Neither abstinence nor partaking has any effect on one's relationship to God.

the meat market. After meat was offered to the idols, it was later sold in the marketplace. At this point, it had no specifically religious connotations and therefore was all right for Christians to buy and eat.

10:26 Psalm 24:1 is used to show that all food belongs to God as the one who ultimately gives it to people. Therefore, no food in itself has any effect on one's relationship to God. What matters is the context in which that food is eaten.

10:27 Paul shifts his focus to the related question of what one might eat or not eat at the home of a non-Christian friend. Paul says that Christians can eat whatever is placed before them in such a setting, although the scruples of one's dinner companions must also be considered.

10:28 *anyone.* It is probably a pagan who points out that what is being offered is idol-food. Pagans viewed Christianity as a Jewish sect, and so assumed Christians followed the same dietary laws.

10:29 *For why should my freedom be judged by another's conscience?* This is Paul's basic point: Christians can eat idol-food freely in homes because they are the Lord's and are not enslaved to anyone else. Under such circumstances, to eat such food would confuse the pagan, implying that the Christian did not take his or her faith seriously.

10:30 As in verse 26, Paul points out that even idol-food comes from God, and is a source of thanksgiving.

10:31 This is a positive restating of what has been put negatively (in vv. 25–30). Use eating and drinking to bring glory to God, not to cause strife or to honor a demon.

10:32 *to stumble.* See also 1 Corinthians 8:13, 9:19–23 and 10:23–24. The word translated "to stumble" probably ought to be translated "to offend" i.e., "try to live without 'offending' in any direction" (Fee).

10:33 *I try to please everybody.* This is Paul's aim, though the hostility of the Corinthians themselves show that he did not always succeed.

> *Christians ought to seek good, not just for their friends, but also for those who are unlike them.*

not seeking my own good. Paul explains what he means. It is not merely a matter of ingratiating oneself with others in order to gain favor or avoid hardship. Rather, his motive is to create openness to the Gospel so that men and women will come to faith.

11:1 *Follow my example.* As an apostle, it was not just his responsibility to teach and preach the Gospel, but to live it out in such a way that people would see what it meant to be a Christian. When establishing new churches, Paul might have been the only Christian new converts had met, and thus their only model.

the example of Christ. For his part, he bases his life on the example of Jesus.

14 Proper Worship—1 Cor. 11:2–16

THREE-PART AGENDA

ICE-BREAKER
15 Minutes

BIBLE STUDY
30 Minutes

CARING TIME
15–45 Minutes

> **LEADER:** Have you started working with your group about your mission—for instance, by having them review page M3 in the center section? If you have a new person at the meeting, remember to do an appropriate ice-breaker from the center section.

TO BEGIN THE BIBLE STUDY TIME
(Choose 1 or 2)

1. On what occasions do you wear a hat? What is your favorite hat or favorite kind of hat to wear?

2. What is the *wildest* hairstyle you ever wore?

3. What "statement" do the kind of clothes you wear make about you?

READ SCRIPTURE & DISCUSS
(If you don't have time for all the questions in this section, conclude the Bible Study [30 min.] by answering question #7.)

1. What teacher has had an impact on your life? What is something they taught you that you still remember?

2. What are your first impressions of this passage? What problem in the Corinthian church is Paul addressing?

3. In this passage, what restrictions does Paul place on the women? On the men? Do any of these Corinthian principles apply to you?

Propriety in Worship

²I praise you for remembering me in everything and for holding to the teachings,[a] *just as I passed them on to you.*

³Now I want you to realize that the head of every man is Christ, and the head of the woman is man, and the head of Christ is God. ⁴Every man who prays or prophesies with his head covered dishonors his head. ⁵And every woman who prays or prophesies with her head uncovered dishonors her head—it is just as though her head were shaved. ⁶If a woman does not cover her head, she should have her hair cut off; and if it is a disgrace for a woman to have her hair cut or shaved off, she should cover her head. ⁷A man ought not to cover his head,[b] *since he is the image and glory of God; but the woman is the glory of man. ⁸For man did not come from woman, but woman from man; ⁹neither was man created for woman, but woman for man. ¹⁰For this reason, and because of the angels, the woman ought to have a sign of authority on her head.*

¹¹In the Lord, however, woman is not independent of man, nor is man independent of woman. ¹²For as woman came from man, so also man is born of woman. But everything comes from God. ¹³Judge for yourselves: Is it proper for a woman to pray to God with her head uncovered? ¹⁴Does not the very nature of things teach you that if a man has long hair, it is a disgrace to him, ¹⁵but that if a woman has long hair, it is her glory? For long hair is given to her as a covering. ¹⁶If anyone wants to be contentious about this, we have no other practice—nor do the churches of God.

[a]2 Or *traditions*
[b]4–7 Or 4 *Every man who prays or prophesies with long hair dishonors his head.* ⁵*And every woman who prays or prophesies with no covering of hair on her head dishonors her head—she is just like one of the "shorn women."* ⁶*If a woman has no covering, let her be for now with short hair, but since it is a disgrace for a woman to have her hair shorn or shaved, she should grow it again.* ⁷*A man ought not to have long hair*

4. What concerns should Christians have today about how they appear in public? In church?

5. In what ways do verses 11 and 12 illustrate our interdependence on each other and God?

6. *Women*: What qualities do men have that women need? *Men*: What qualities do women have that men need? *All*: What does God have that we need?

7. Many things in our worship reflect the culture we live in (type of music, style of dress, etc.). How do you discern when a cultural practice is okay and when it is a hindrance to worship? How can you best prepare yourself for worship this week?

CARING TIME

(Choose 1 or 2 of these questions before closing in prayer. Be sure to pray for the empty chair.)

1. What is your dream for the future mission for this group?

2. If this group is helping to hold you accountable for something, how are you doing in that area? If not, what is something for which you would like this group to help hold you accountable?

3. What is one specific thing you would like this group to pray about for you?

Summary. Paul tackles another question raised in the letter sent him by the Corinthians (7:1): the veiling of women. This is the first of a series of problems (in chapters 11–14) related to conduct at worship services. This section is *not* about wives submitting to husbands, or women trying to act like men. Such misunderstanding may arise since Paul's argument here is notoriously difficult to follow "... because he is convinced that the women should continue the prevailing custom (of wearing veils). But to get them to do so he must give some good reasons. Therefore, the argument fluctuates from one reason to another, but not in clearly distinguishable paragraphs" (Fee).

11:2 *I praise you.* Paul has been forced to say some hard things to the Corinthian Christians, but he is by no means unequivocally negative toward them. Whenever possible he praises them. Here, specifically, he praises them for thinking kindly of him (perhaps only a portion of the church chafed under his "restrictions" or perhaps he is being slightly tongue-in-cheek here). He also praises them for adhering to basic Christian teaching.

teachings. Literally, "traditions." Since the New Testament had not yet been compiled, Paul instructed his converts in the Christian way of life by word-of-mouth in accord with the practices of those who were in Christ before him. It is clear in verses 3–16, however, that they were breaking the tradition regarding women veiling themselves in worship.

11:3 *head.* The key word in this section, used some 12 times. The difficulty is that Paul sometimes uses the word literally (referring to the physical head—i.e., in vv. 4a, 5a, 5c, 6, 7, 10). However, in verse 3, "head" is used metaphorically. And in verse 4b and verse 5b, it is not clear which sense is intended (though it is probably metaphorical)! Such wordplay is not unusual in Paul's writings.

the head of the woman is man. While today (and in the Old Testament) "head" might be understood to mean "the ruler of a community," in Greek, when the word is used metaphorically, it generally means "origin," as in the "source (head) of a river." What Paul has in mind here (as is clear from vv. 8–9) is Genesis 2:18–23—the creation of the first woman from the first man. Woman has her *origins* in man. Had Paul wanted to convey the idea of man ruling

over woman, he would have used a different Greek word (Barrett).

the head of Christ is God. God is the origin and therefore the explanation of Christ's being, just as Christ is the creating agent of all people.

11:4 *prophesies.* Paul will discuss the gift of prophecy in chapter 14.

with his head covered. This most likely refers to a veil that covered the whole head down to the shoulders, such as respectable Jewish and Roman women wore in public. It does not refer to a hat or a kerchief. In fact, it was the custom for Jewish men, not women, to wear a small cap when at worship.

dishonors his head. Probably this use of "head" is metaphorical and refers to Christ. A man with his head covered dishonors Christ.

11:5 *with her head uncovered.* It is difficult to know the nature of the local custom, but what is clear is that women were participating actively in public worship (praying and prophesying), that they were doing so without a veil, and that this was offensive. Note that Paul does not forbid participation by women in worship. If this were wrong in and of itself, he would have simply told them to stop. He would not have wasted time telling them to wear veils.

dishonors her head. Probably the second use of "head" is metaphorical here (as in v. 4). A woman shames her husband when she is unveiled during worship.

11:6 Since Paul understands that nature dictates a covering of hair for a woman (vv. 14–15), it is as unnatural an act for her to go without a veil as it is for her to have her hair shaved off. This argument is cultural in nature. In the same way that she would be disgraced by shaving off her hair, she is disgraced by not having a veil when praying and prophesying.

11:7 Arguing from the order of origin in verse 3, here Paul gives his conclusion as it applies to veils. "Men should not be covered in divine worship because that would cover 'Christ's glory,' which is seen in man. And Christ's glory should be seen. But the wife should be covered—to be uncovered would mean to reflect 'man's glory,' which is seen in women. And one should not call attention to the creature in the presence of the Creator in worship" (Fee).

11:8–9 Paul explains in what sense the woman is the glory of man.

11:10 *For this reason.* This refers back to verse 7. The reason why a woman is to wear a veil on her head is because man's glory should not be exposed during worship. He also offers two more reasons why a woman should wear a veil (because of angels and because it is a sign of her new authority).

because of the angels. Angels were seen as the "guardians of the created order" and as such would be offended by this "lapse from due order."

a sign of authority. Since now a woman, as well as a man, " 'speaks to God in prayer and declares his word in prophecy, to do so she needs authority and power from God. The head covering which symbolizes the effacement of man's glory in the presence of God also serves as a sign of the authority which is given to the woman.' That is, her veil represents the new authority given to women under the new dispensation to do things which formerly had not been permitted her" (Hooker in Barrett).

11:11 *however.* In verses 11–12, Paul balances what he said in verses 8–9. Though woman came from man (Gen. 2:21 says she was taken from Adam's side), it is also true that men come from women in the natural course of childbirth. Men and women are mutually interdependent.

not independent. While verses 2–16 do not directly examine the relationship between husband and wife, here Paul does point out the mutual interdependence that exists between men and women and their equal dependence on God.

11:13–15 Paul now argues on the basis of the cultural norms of that day (whereby it was felt that it was proper for men to have short hair and proper for women to have long hair). Thus, from the culture's point of view, it was a disgrace for a woman to pray without a veil.

> *Though woman came from man, it is also true that men come from women in the natural course of childbirth. Men and women are mutually interdependent.*

11:14 *the very nature of things.* Paul argues that men should have short hair, not because "nature" dictates that male hair is short. In fact, "nature" dictates that all hair grows constantly. It is culture (this is what "the very nature of things" means) that dictates that male hair ought to be cut, and it is custom that dictates that shame comes when it is not.

11:16 The conclusion of Paul's argument is: "This is the way it has always been done, and to attempt otherwise is to bring dissension into the church, and that clearly is not good." He seems to be saying to the church that they ought not to call attention to themselves by disregarding this particular cultural norm.

15 Lord's Supper—1 Cor. 11:17–34

THREE-PART AGENDA

ICE-BREAKER
15 Minutes

BIBLE STUDY
30 Minutes

CARING TIME
15–45 Minutes

LEADER: If there's a new person in this session, start with an ice-breaker from the center section (see page M7). Remember to stick closely to the three-part agenda. You may want to celebrate the Lord's Supper as a group in place of the usual Caring Time.

TO BEGIN THE BIBLE STUDY TIME
(Choose 1 or 2)

1. What's your favorite place to eat?

2. When you were growing up, what was dinner time like? Who sat where around the table?

3. How is the Lord's Supper observed in your church and how often?

READ SCRIPTURE & DISCUSS
(If you don't have time for all the questions in this section, conclude the Bible Study [30 min.] by answering question #7.)

1. When has the Lord's Supper been particularly meaningful to you?

2. How would you describe the scene if you were observing the Lord's Supper at the Corinthian church?

3. Have you ever been in a church that was affected by divisions among the members? How did that affect the worship services?

The Lord's Supper

17In the following directives I have no praise for you, for your meetings do more harm than good. 18In the first place, I hear that when you come together as a church, there are divisions among you, and to some extent I believe it. 19No doubt there have to be differences among you to show which of you have God's approval. 20When you come together, it is not the Lord's Supper you eat, 21for as you eat, each of you goes ahead without waiting for anybody else. One remains hungry, another gets drunk. 22Don't you have homes to eat and drink in? Or do you despise the church of God and humiliate those who have nothing? What shall I say to you? Shall I praise you for this? Certainly not!

23For I received from the Lord what I also passed on to you: The Lord Jesus, on the night he was betrayed, took bread, 24and when he had given thanks, he broke it and said, "This is my body, which is for you; do this in remembrance of me." 25In the same way, after supper he took the cup, saying, "This cup is the new covenant in my blood; do this, whenever you drink it, in remembrance of me." 26For whenever you eat this bread and drink this cup, you proclaim the Lord's death until he comes.

27Therefore, whoever eats the bread or drinks the cup of the Lord in an unworthy manner will be guilty of sinning against the body and blood of the Lord. 28A man ought to examine himself before he eats of the bread and drinks of the cup. 29For anyone who eats and drinks without recognizing the body of the Lord eats and drinks judgment on himself. 30That is why many among you are weak and sick, and a number of you have fallen asleep. 31But if we judged ourselves, we would not come under judgment. 32When we are judged by the Lord, we are being disciplined so that we will not be condemned with the world.

33So then, my brothers, when you come together to eat, wait for each other. 34If anyone is hungry, he should eat at home, so that when you meet together it may not result in judgment.

And when I come I will give further directions.

4. Paul repeats the words used during the Lord's Supper in verses 23–26. How do you respond when you hear these words during Communion?

5. In this passage, Paul instructs the Corinthians to examine themselves prior to partaking of the Lord's Supper. How is this done? What are the consequences of receiving the Lord's Supper "in an unworthy manner" (v. 27)?

6. Why is it important for Christians to observe the Lord's Supper? What does Communion mean to you?

7. What can you do to best prepare yourself before you next receive the Lord's Supper?

CARING TIME

(Choose 1 or 2 of these questions before closing in prayer. Be sure to pray for the empty chair.)

1. What's something you are looking forward to this week?

2. Share a spiritual struggle or victory from this last week.

3. How can the group pray for you this week?

Summary. Paul turns to a second, more serious disorder in the Corinthians' worship experience: their abuse of the Lord's Supper. The Lord's Supper was eaten in the context of a community meal—a so-called "love feast" (Jude 12). The problem was that the way they behaved at this meal accented their divisions (rich and poor, followers of one or another leader, etc.) rather than affirmed their unity in Christ.

11:17 *more harm than good.* In fact, so flawed are their Communion services that they would be better off not having them. They harm, not heal.

11:18 *I hear.* They had *not* written Paul about these disorders. Paul had heard what was going on from other sources (see 1 Cor. 1:11; 16:17), and is so shocked that he can't really believe that it is as bad as reported ("to some extent I believe it").

church. This word originally referred to a group of citizens who had assembled together for a predetermined purpose. In the Greek Old Testament, this word was used to describe the assembling together of God's people, and it came to have this meaning in the New Testament as well.

divisions. It seems that class distinction operated at the Lord's Supper—the rich ate abundantly while the poor were hungry. It is also possible that Jewish Christians ate kosher food by themselves apart from Gentile Christians, and that the ascetics sat apart from the libertarians, that those who followed Apollos did not mingle with those who followed Cephas, etc.

11:19 This may be intended as sarcasm. Since each group assumes they are the ones with "God's approval," no wonder they separate from each other. On the other hand, he may mean that those who are acting in a truly Christian fashion have become quite obvious by comparison with all the others!

11:20 *it is not the Lord's Supper you eat.* The Corinthians have so badly abused the Communion service that it was more like one of the meals at a pagan temple than a meal held in honor of the Lord.

11:21 *goes ahead without waiting for anybody else.* Apparently, the poor were actually being excluded from the Lord's Supper (v. 33). It is conjectured that the "nobodies" who made up much of the church (1:26) were in fact slaves (7:20–24), and so did not have the freedom to get to church when they wanted to, and the others just weren't waiting for them (Fee).

hungry / drunk. The contrast could not be more stark. The poor in the church went hungry during this meal, while others indulged themselves to the point of drunkenness!

11:22 If the rich can't wait to indulge in their food and drink, at least they should do this at home and not demean the common meal at church.

humiliate those who have nothing. The poor feel ashamed that they can't bring the abundant food and drink they see the rich eating. Paul's point is that God accepts the poor, so the rich ought not to make them feel unworthy.

11:23–26 To correct this unacceptable situation, Paul repeats the tradition of the Lord's Supper (later incorporated in the Gospels: Matthew 26:26–28; Mark 14:22–24; Luke 22:19–20) which provides the pattern for how the Corinthians should conduct their Communion service.

11:23 *on the night he was betrayed.* The significance of what Jesus did at the Last Supper comes in the context of *when* it took place—immediately prior to his crucifixion.

11:24 *thanks.* There is nothing unusual in this act. The head of each Jewish household would have done the same thing.

This is my body. Then Jesus interprets for the disciples the new meaning he is giving to these ordinary acts. He himself will become the Passover lamb for them, to be slain for their sins.

> *The shedding of Jesus' blood inaugurates a new covenant between God and people by which their sins are forgiven as a result of Christ's death in their place.*

in remembrance. Paul repeats this phrase twice, so as to stress that the Lord's Supper is a memorial feast (see Luke 22:19).

11:25 in my blood. The shedding of Jesus' blood inaugurates a new covenant between God and people by which their sins are forgiven as a result of Christ's death in their place.

11:26 This statement is not found in the Gospels. It is Paul's own summary of the meaning of the Lord's Supper.

proclaim the Lord's death. The Lord's Supper proclaims the fact and meaning of Jesus' death in several ways: the broken bread and outpoured wine symbolically proclaim his death; the words spoken at such a meal (both formally and informally) recall the Crucifixion; and the whole event itself "proclaims" his atoning death. This is why the abuses by the Corinthians are so appalling. Added together, they proclaimed a false gospel.

until he comes. In this way, Christians recall the story of Jesus' death until he returns.

11:27–34 The problem Paul addresses has two parts: the vertical and the horizontal. "The vertical part of the problem was their failure to honor the Lord. The horizontal part of the problem was their failure to eat the meal as a loving community" (Fee). Paul has just dealt with the vertical (theological) problem in verses 23–26. Now, in verses 27–34, he deals with the horizontal (relational) problem which he outlined in verses 17–22.

11:27 in an unworthy manner. This refers to the disorders in community behavior (vv. 18–22). They are to scrutinize their lives to see if they are contributing to the divisiveness of the community.

11:28 to examine himself. Christians ought to scrutinize their lives to see if they are guilty of divisiveness, of lack of love, of gluttony and drunkenness (i.e., the Corinthian disorders) which might reflect negatively on "the body and the blood of the Lord." Moral perfection is not required, simply moral scrutiny.

11:29 without recognizing. When the meal turned into a time of drunkenness, division and gluttony, people lost sight of the meaning of the event.

the body of the Lord. "The words 'of the Lord' are almost certainly not in the original text. They are missing from the best early manuscripts" (Fee). Here, "the body" in view is probably the church (as in 12:12), which the Corinthians were abusing. Thus they would come under the judgment Paul warned about in regard to those who defiled God's temple, the church (3:17).

11:30 Paul contends that the judgment in verse 29 works itself out in concrete, physical ways. "Those who abused the Lord's table were exposing themselves to the power of demons, who were taken to be the cause of physical disease. This verse is first an explanation of events known to be taking place in Corinth, and secondly a threat directed against those who continued to misuse the Supper" (Barrett).

> Christians ought to scrutinize their lives to see if they are guilty of divisiveness, of lack of love, of gluttony and drunkenness which might reflect negatively on "the body and the blood of the Lord." Moral perfection is not required, simply moral scrutiny.

fallen asleep. A figure of speech for death.

11:31–32 Self-evaluation (and change) is the way to avoid the judgment from God.

11:32 This judgment may not, in the end, turn out to be so bad, because discipline yields growth.

11:33–34 In these exhortations, Paul sums up verses 17–32.

11:34 further directions. Paul has apparently dealt with only the most serious problems connected with the celebration of the Lord's Supper. The other areas can wait until his visit.

16 Spiritual Gifts—1 Cor. 12:1–31a

THREE-PART AGENDA

ICE-BREAKER
15 Minutes

BIBLE STUDY
30 Minutes

CARING TIME
15–45 Minutes

 LEADER: *If you haven't already, now is the time to begin the process of identifying an Apprentice / Leader to start a new small group (see page M6 in the center section). Check the list of ice-breakers on page M7, especially if you have a new person in this session.*

TO BEGIN THE BIBLE STUDY TIME
(Choose 1 or 2)

1. What is one of your favorite sights or smells?

2. Growing up, what was the best gift you ever received?

3. What "hidden" talent do you have that others in this group might not know about?

READ SCRIPTURE & DISCUSS
(If you don't have time for all the questions in this section, conclude the Bible Study [30 min.] by answering question #7.)

1. When have you felt that you were part of a unit where all the parts worked together for a common goal?

2. Who has been given spiritual gifts? Who are they from and for what purpose are they given (v. 7)?

3. Verses 4–6 indicate the probability that some Corinthians might have believed that their possession of certain spiritual gifts made them better than those believers who did not possess the same gift. Have you ever encountered that attitude among Christians? Have you ever had the same attitude about your own spiritual condition?

12 *Now about spiritual gifts, brothers, I do not want you to be ignorant. ²You know that when you were pagans, somehow or other you were influenced and led astray to mute idols. ³Therefore I tell you that no one who is speaking by the Spirit of God says, "Jesus be cursed," and no one can say, "Jesus is Lord," except by the Holy Spirit.*

⁴There are different kinds of gifts, but the same Spirit. ⁵There are different kinds of service, but the same Lord. ⁶There are different kinds of working, but the same God works all of them in all men.

⁷Now to each one the manifestation of the Spirit is given for the common good. ⁸To one there is given through the Spirit the message of wisdom, to another the message of knowledge by means of the same Spirit, ⁹to another faith by the same Spirit, to another gifts of healing by that one Spirit, ¹⁰to another miraculous powers, to another prophecy, to another distinguishing between spirits, to another speaking in different kinds of tongues,ᵃ and to still another the interpretation of tongues.ᵃ ¹¹All these are the work of one and the same Spirit, and he gives them to each one, just as he determines.

One Body, Many Parts

¹²The body is a unit, though it is made up of many parts; and though all its parts are many, they form one body. So it is with Christ. ¹³For we were all baptized byᵇ one Spirit into one body—whether Jews or Greeks, slave or free—and we were all given the one Spirit to drink.

¹⁴Now the body is not made up of one part but of many. ¹⁵If the foot should say, "Because I am not a hand, I do not belong to the body," it would not for that reason cease to be part of the body. ¹⁶And if the ear should say, "Because I am not an eye, I do not belong to the body," it would not for that reason cease to be part of the body. ¹⁷If the whole body were an eye, where would the sense of hearing be? If the whole body were an ear, where would the sense of smell be? ¹⁸But in fact God has arranged the parts in the body, every one of them, just as he wanted them to be. ¹⁹If they

4. Describe yourself as a "part" of the body of Christ (an eye, hand, etc.). Why did you select that part?

5. Read verse 26. How good are you at hurting with a fellow believer who is suffering and rejoicing with a fellow believer who is honored? Which comes easier for you?

6. How connected are you to your church body? What could you do to help "the body" function better?

7. How do you (or could you) use your gifts and abilities within the church? What holds you back from using your gifts more fully?

CARING TIME
(Choose 1 or 2 of these questions before closing in prayer. Be sure to pray for the empty chair.)

1. What gifts or "body parts" (e.g. an ear [good listener], etc.) do you see in this group?

2. What was the best thing that happened to you this last week?

3. How can the group help you in prayer this week?

were all one part, where would the body be? ²⁰As it is, there are many parts, but one body.

²¹The eye cannot say to the hand, "I don't need you!" And the head cannot say to the feet, "I don't need you!" ²²On the contrary, those parts of the body that seem to be weaker are indispensable, ²³and the parts that we think are less honorable we treat with special honor. And the parts that are unpresentable are treated with special modesty, ²⁴while our presentable parts need no special treatment. But God has combined the members of the body and has given greater honor to the parts that lacked it, ²⁵so that there should be no division in the body, but that its parts should have equal concern for each other. ²⁶If one part suffers, every part suffers with it; if one part is honored, every part rejoices with it.

²⁷Now you are the body of Christ, and each one of you is a part of it. ²⁸And in the church God has appointed first of all apostles, second prophets, third teachers, then workers of miracles, also those having gifts of healing, those able to help others, those with gifts of administration, and those speaking in different kinds of tongues. ²⁹Are all apostles? Are all prophets? Are all teachers? Do all work miracles? ³⁰Do all have gifts of healing? Do all speak in tongues^c? Do all interpret? ³¹But eagerly desire^d the greater gifts.

---

^{a}10 Or *languages,* also in verse 28 ^{b}13 Or *with;* or *in* ^{c}30 Or *other languages*
^{d}31 Or *But you are eagerly desiring*

Notes—1 Corinthians 12:1–31a

Summary. In chapters 12–14, Paul deals with the third and final issue related to the worship experience of the Corinthian church: the abuse of the gift of tongues. His emphasis here in the first section (12:1–11) is on the variety of gifts given by the Spirit, over against the Corinthians' preoccupation with one particular gift.

12:1 *Now about.* Paul responds to yet another concern voiced in their letter.

12:2–3 Paul contrasts pagan and Christian ecstasy. The difference is not the experience of ecstasy, but who inspires the ecstasy—the Holy Spirit or another (demonic) spirit. The identity of the inspiring source is known by the content of the utterance. The Holy Spirit exalts Jesus Christ.

12:2 *influenced and led astray.* The image is of the ecstasy within pagan religion, where one was possessed (or thought to be) and "carried away" by a supernatural being.

mute idols. The idols in themselves were nothing, they were silent (they could not answer prayer); but behind them lay very real demonic powers.

12:3 *speaking by.* The idea of speech directly inspired by the Spirit of God. The question is not whether such ecstatic speech occurs (Paul assumes that it does), but what is the *content* of the speech. "Not the manner but the content of ecstatic speech determines its authenticity" (Barrett).

"Jesus be cursed." It is not clear who would have uttered such words, or under what conditions.

"Jesus is Lord." To be able to confess that one is the servant of Jesus who is indeed Lord (Master, King) of the universe is a sign of the Holy Spirit at work.

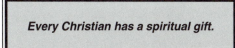

Every Christian has a spiritual gift.

12:4–6 Paul points out that not all Christians have the same gift (nor every gift), nor do they render the same service. However, all gifts spring from the same Spirit, are used to serve the same Lord, and

are all energized by the power of the same God. (This is an early statement of the Trinity.)

12:5 *service.* The purpose of the gifts is to serve and aid others in various ways, yet all is done in the name of and for the sake of the same Lord.

12:6 *working.* The Greek root is *energeia* ("energy"), and refers to the various ways in which God's power is displayed in the gifts.

12:7 *to each one.* Every Christian has a spiritual gift.

for the common good. The purpose of these gifts is not private advantage, but community growth.

12:8–10 Paul illustrates th variety of gifts. By chapter 14 it will have become clear that he stresses this point because the Corinthians had become preoccupied, to their detriment, with a single gift—tongues.

12:8 *through the Spirit.* Paul again emphasizes the supernatural origins of these gifts.

wisdom / knowledge. It is not clear how (or if) these gifts differ. Perhaps a message of wisdom focused on practical, ethical instruction, while a message of knowledge involved exposition of biblical truth. In either case, the emphasis is on the actual discourse given for the benefit of the assembled Christians.

12:9 *faith.* Special ability "to claim from God extraordinary manifestations of power in the natural world" (Barrett). Saving faith, which all Christians share, is not in view here.

healing. Special ability to effect miraculous cures. Paul apparently had this gift (Acts 14:8–10).

12:10 *miraculous powers.* Probably the gift of exorcism and similar types of confrontation with evil supernatural powers.

prophecy. Inspired utterances given in ordinary (not ecstatic) speech, distinguished from teaching and wisdom by its unpremeditated nature.

distinguishing between spirits. Just because a person claimed to be inspired by the Holy Spirit did not make it true. Those who possessed this gift of discernment were able to identify the source of an utterance—whether it came from the Holy Spirit or another spirit.

tongues. Ecstatic speech, unintelligible except by those with the gift of interpretation of tongues.

interpretation of tongues. This gift allowed a person to understand and explain to others what was being said by someone else in a tongue.

12:11 Paul underscores his main point: the gifts are given by the Spirit's choice and for his purposes. Hence, they are not a sign of spiritual attainment.

12:12–31 Having pointed out the diversity of gifts in 12:1–11, now Paul examines the unity that exists within all this diversity. After stating that Christians are all part of one body (vv. 12–13), Paul returns to the idea of diversity, in which he not only points out the variety of gifts that exist, but the fact that none are inferior and all are necessary.

12:12 *a unit ... made up of many parts.* This is Paul's central point in verses 12–30: "diversity within unity."

So it is with Christ. The church is the body of Christ (v. 27), and so indeed Christ can be understood to be made up of many parts. Yet he is also the Lord (v. 3), and thus head over that church.

12:13 Here Paul points to the unity side of the body of Christ. Unity exists because all were baptized into one Spirit, and all drink from one Spirit. His concern is not with how people become believers, but with how believers become one body. The term "baptism" is probably metaphorical (Fee). The way believers are "put into one Spirit" is like baptism; i.e., "think of it as being immersed in the Spirit."

baptized by one Spirit. In fact, the NIV footnoted translation of the preposition is probably the correct rendering: "baptized in one Spirit," since Paul's concern is not with the means by which believers are baptized, but with the common reality in which all believers exist; i.e., the Holy Spirit (Fee).

one Spirit to drink. Paul continues speaking metaphorically, with the idea of water still dominant.

Being incorporated into one body is not only like baptism, it is also like "drinking the same Spirit."

12:14 Now Paul points to the diversity side of the body of Christ (which is his major concern): the one body has many different parts to it.

12:15–26 Having established that all Christians are part of one body (which is, in fact, Christ's body) and that this body has a variety of parts, Paul then develops an elaborate metaphor based on the human body. He makes two points: There are a variety of gifts (vv. 15–20), and each gift is vital, regardless of its nature (vv. 21–26).

12:15–20 It is just as ludicrous for Christians to opt out of the body of Christ (presumably by not using their gifts during worship) because they have one gift and not another (presumably more desired) gift, as it is for a foot (or ear) to decide not to be a part of a physical body because it is not a hand (or eye).

> *The church is the body of Christ, and so indeed Christ can be understood to be made up of many parts. Yet he is also the Lord, and thus head over that church.*

12:17 If all Christians had the same gift, the body would be impoverished.

12:21–26 Just as it is presumptuous of the eye (or head) to say to the hand (or foot) that it has no need of it, so too, a Christian ought not to deny the value, need or function of anyone's spiritual gift, especially on the basis that it is different from (or inferior to) one's own gift.

12:21 Each part of the body needs the other parts. No one gift (e.g., tongues) can stand alone. Wholeness in the body requires that all the parts function together.

12:22 *weaker.* "The delicate organs, such as the eye; and the invisible organs, such as the heart" (Barrett).

12:26 In fact, the whole person suffers when one (to use a modern example) sprains an ankle. It is not just the ankle that suffers.

12:27 Paul sums up the meaning of his metaphor.

the body of Christ. By this phrase, Paul conveys the idea not that Christ consists of this body, but that Christ rules over this body, and that this body belongs to him.

12:28 Paul offers a second list of the types of gifts given by the Holy Spirit (see the parallel list in Eph. 4:11)—mixing together ministries (e.g., apostles) with spiritual gifts (e.g., the gift of healing).

apostles. These individuals were responsible for founding new churches. They were pioneer church planters.

prophets. Those who were inspired to speak God's word to the church, in plain (not ecstatic) language.

teachers. Those gifted to instruct others in the meaning of the Christian faith and its implications for one's life.

then. Having first focused on those gifts whereby the church is established and nurtured, Paul then shifts to other gifts.

to help others. The gift of support; those whose function it was to aid the needy (e.g., the poor, the widow, the orphan).

administration. The gift of direction (literally, the process of steering a ship through the rocks and safely to shore); those whose function it was to guide church affairs.

> *If all Christians had the same gift, the body would be impoverished.*

12:29–30 While Paul does not rule out the possibility that a particular individual might possess more than one gift, he is quite clear that no one has all the gifts. The implied answer to each question is "No."

12:31 *the greater gifts.* These are the gifts which edify the church most. Paul establishes the context within which all gifts should function: love, which is the more excellent way.

THREE-PART AGENDA

ICE-BREAKER
15 Minutes

BIBLE STUDY
30 Minutes

CARING TIME
15–45 Minutes

> **LEADER:** *To help you identify an Apprentice / Leader for a new small group (or if you have a new person at this meeting), see the listing of appropriate ice-breakers on page M7 of the center section.*

TO BEGIN THE BIBLE STUDY TIME
(Choose 1 or 2)

1. Who was your first "true love"? Was it infatuation or the real thing?

2. What is your favorite love song, poem or romantic movie?

3. When it comes to sacrificial and unconditional love, who would you nominate to be in the "Hall of Fame"?

READ SCRIPTURE & DISCUSS
(If you don't have time for all the questions in this section, conclude the Bible Study [30 min.] by answering question #7.)

1. When in your life have you felt the most loved? How did that love affect your life?

2. In verses 1–3, what activities are useless without love?

3. In this passage, what does Paul say love is? What does Paul say love is not?

4. How does love as described in this chapter compare to love as typically defined in our culture?

Love

And now I will show you the most excellent way.

13 **If I speak in the tongues^a of men and of angels, but have not love, I am only a resounding gong or a clanging cymbal. ²If I have the gift of prophecy and can fathom all mysteries and all knowledge, and if I have a faith that can move mountains, but have not love, I am nothing. ³If I give all I possess to the poor and surrender my body to the flames,^b but have not love, I gain nothing.**

⁴Love is patient, love is kind. It does not envy, it does not boast, it is not proud. ⁵It is not rude, it is not self-seeking, it is not easily angered, it keeps no record of wrongs. ⁶Love does not delight in evil but rejoices with the truth. ⁷It always protects, always trusts, always hopes, always perseveres.

⁸Love never fails. But where there are prophecies, they will cease; where there are tongues, they will be stilled; where there is knowledge, it will pass away. ⁹For we know in part and we prophesy in part, ¹⁰but when perfection comes, the imperfect disappears. ¹¹When I was a child, I talked like a child, I thought like a child, I reasoned like a child. When I became a man, I put childish ways behind me. ¹²Now we see but a poor reflection as in a mirror; then we shall see face to face. Now I know in part; then I shall know fully, even as I am fully known.

¹³And now these three remain: faith, hope and love. But the greatest of these is love.

^a1 Or *languages*   ^b3 Some early manuscripts *body that I may boast*

5. Looking at the descriptions of perfect love in verses 4–7, in which one of these descriptions are you strongest? In which one are you weakest?

6. How does it make you feel that you are "fully known" (v. 12) by God?

7. What can you do for someone at home or at work that would make these qualities of love come to life in a practical way?

CARING TIME

(Choose 1 or 2 of these questions before closing in prayer. Be sure to pray for the empty chair.)

1. Have you started working on your group mission—to choose an Apprentice / Leader from this group to start a new group in the future? (See Mission / Multiplication on page M3.)

2. What is something you did this last week to help you grow in your faith?

3. How can the group support you in prayer this week?

Summary. In this soaring hymn in praise of love (which has become a classic piece of literature), Paul points out (vv. 1–3) the primacy of love (in contrast to other religious activities), describes love itself (vv. 4–7), and ends (vv. 8–13) by pointing out love's enduring quality (in contrast, once again, to other religious activities). As Karl Barth outlines the chapter: "It is love alone that counts (vv. 1–3); it is love alone that triumphs (vv. 4–7); it is love alone that endures (vv. 8–13)."

13:1–3 If a person does not love, neither spiritual gifts, nor good deeds, nor martyrdom is of any ultimate value to that person. Love is the context within which these gifts and deeds become significant.

13:1 *tongues of men and of angels.* Ecstatic speech—highly prized in Corinth—is an authentic gift of the Holy Spirit. However, it becomes like the unintelligible noise of pagan worship when used outside the context of love.

gong / cymbal. Paul is probably thinking of the repetitious and meaningless noise generated at pagan temples by beating on metal instruments.

13:2 Paul contrasts three other spiritual gifts with love: prophecy, knowledge and faith.

prophecy. Such activity is highly commended by Paul (e.g., 14:1), yet without love a prophet is really nothing.

fathom all mysteries. In Corinth, special and esoteric knowledge was highly valued (1:18–2:16); but even if one knew the very secrets of God, without love it would be to no end. That which makes a person significant (i.e., the opposite of "nothing") is not a gift like prophecy or knowledge, but the ability to love.

faith that can move mountains. Paul refers to Jesus' words in Mark 11:23—even such massive faith that can unleash God's power in visible ways is not enough to make a person significant without love at its foundation.

13:3 *give all I possess to the poor.* Presumably Paul refers to goods and property given to others, but not in love. The point is not: do not give if you cannot do so in love (the poor still profit from gifts, regardless of the spirit in which they are given), but rather that the loveless giver gains no reward on the Day of Judgment.

surrender my body. Not even martyrdom—giving up one's life for the sake of another or in a great cause—brings personal benefit when it is done outside love.

13:4–7 Paul says what love does and does not do. He defines love in terms of action and attitude.

13:4 *patient.* This word describes patience with people (not circumstances). It characterizes the person who is slow to anger (long-suffering) despite provocation.

> *If a person does not love, neither spiritual gifts, nor good deeds, nor martyrdom is of any ultimate value to that person. Love is the context within which these gifts and deeds become significant.*

kind. The loving person does good to others.

not envy. The loving person does not covet what others have, nor begrudge them their possessions.

not boast. The loving person is self-effacing, not a braggart.

not proud. Literally, not "puffed up." The loving person does not feel others to be inferior, nor looks down on people.

13:5 *not rude.* The same Greek word is used in 1 Corinthians 7:36 to describe a man who led on a woman, but then refused to marry her.

not self-seeking. Loving people not only do not insist on their rights, but will give up their due for the sake of others.

not easily angered. Loving people are not easily angered by others; they are not touchy.

keeps no record of wrongs. The verb is an accounting term, and the image is of a ledger sheet on which wrongs received are recorded. The loving person forgives and forgets.

13:6 does not delight in evil. Loving people do not rejoice when others fail (which could make them feel superior), nor enjoy pointing out the wrong in others.

rejoices with the truth. Paul shifts back to the positive.

protects. Literally, "to put a cover over." The loving person is concerned with how to shelter other people from harm.

13:7 trusts. Literally, "believes all things"; i.e., "never loses faith."

hopes. Love "stubbornly adheres to the conviction that life has purpose and meaning" (Orr/Walther).

perseveres. Love keeps loving despite hardship.

13:8–12 Having described love, Paul once again contrasts love with spiritual gifts. This time, the apostle wants to emphasize the permanent quality of love over against the transitory nature of the gifts (*charismata*).

13:8 Love never fails. In the sense that it functions both now and in the age to come. Spiritual gifts are relevant only to this age.

cease / be stilled / pass away. One day, when Christ comes again in fullness, prophecy will be fulfilled (and so cease), the indirect communication with God via tongues will no longer be needed (so they are stilled), and since all will be revealed and be evident, secret knowledge about God will be redundant (and so will pass away). Each of these are partial revelations about God, vital in this present age, but unnecessary in the age to come.

13:11 The contrast is between this age (when we are still children) and the age to come (when we are mature).

13:12 Now / then. Paul is thinking of the Second Coming. The here-and-now experience is contrasted to that when Christ's kingdom is revealed in its fullness.

> *Charismatic gifts will cease, because they bring only partial knowledge of God; but three things will carry over into the new age: faith, hope and love.*

poor reflection. Corinth was famous for the mirrors it made out of highly polished metal. Still, no mirror manufactured in the first century was without imperfections. All of them distorted the image somewhat, and so this is an apt metaphor for the present knowledge of God—it is marred (until the day we see the Lord clearly in heaven).

13:13 remain. Charismatic gifts will cease, because they bring only partial knowledge of God; but three things will carry over into the new age: faith, hope and love.

the greatest of these is love. Because God is love (1 John 4:8). After everything else is no longer necessary, love will still be the governing principle.

THREE-PART AGENDA

ICE-BREAKER
15 Minutes

BIBLE STUDY
30 Minutes

CARING TIME
15–45 Minutes

 LEADER: How is the group progressing on reaching its mission goal? Does the group need to review pages M3 and M6 in the center section? If you have a new person at the meeting, remember to do an ice-breaker from the center section.

TO BEGIN THE BIBLE STUDY TIME
(Choose 1 or 2)

1. What sound or noise do you like or dislike?

2. Growing up, what musical instrument did you play? What instrument do you (or would you like to) play now?

3. When have you been some place where you didn't understand the language? How did you feel?

READ SCRIPTURE & DISCUSS
(If you don't have time for all the questions in this section, conclude the Bible Study [30 min.] by answering question #7.)

1. In what ways have you experienced the power and presence of God in your life?

2. What problem is Paul addressing in this passage? Why might this have been a problem in the Corinthian church?

3. What is the difference between speaking in tongues and prophesying, and in what sense is prophecy better than tongues (vv. 2–5)?

Gifts of Prophecy and Tongues

14 *Follow the way of love and eagerly desire spiritual gifts, especially the gift of prophecy. [2] For anyone who speaks in a tongue[a] does not speak to men but to God. Indeed, no one understands him; he utters mysteries with his spirit.[b] [3] But everyone who prophesies speaks to men for their strengthening, encouragement and comfort. [4] He who speaks in a tongue edifies himself, but he who prophesies edifies the church. [5] I would like every one of you to speak in tongues,[c] but I would rather have you prophesy. He who prophesies is greater than one who speaks in tongues,[c] unless he interprets, so that the church may be edified.*

[6] Now, brothers, if I come to you and speak in tongues, what good will I be to you, unless I bring you some revelation or knowledge or prophecy or word of instruction? [7] Even in the case of lifeless things that make sounds, such as the flute or harp, how will anyone know what tune is being played unless there is a distinction in the notes? [8] Again, if the trumpet does not sound a clear call, who will get ready for battle? [9] So it is with you. Unless you speak intelligible words with your tongue, how will anyone know what you are saying? You will just be speaking into the air. [10] Undoubtedly there are all sorts of languages in the world, yet none of them is without meaning. [11] If then I do not grasp the meaning of what someone is saying, I am a foreigner to the speaker, and he is a foreigner to me. [12] So it is with you. Since you are eager to have spiritual gifts, try to excel in gifts that build up the church.

[13] For this reason anyone who speaks in a tongue should pray that he may interpret what he says. [14] For if I pray in a tongue, my spirit prays, but my mind is unfruitful. [15] So what shall I do? I will pray with my spirit, but I will also pray with my mind; I will sing with my spirit, but I will also sing with my mind. [16] If you are praising God with your spirit, how can one who finds himself among those who do not understand[d] say "Amen" to your thanksgiving, since he does not know what you are saying? [17] You may be giving thanks well enough, but the other man is not edified.

[18] I thank God that I speak in tongues more than all of you. [19] But in the church I would rather speak five intelligible

4. What corrective instructions does Paul repeat throughout this passage?

5. The Corinthians might have been partial to ecstatic or flamboyant spirituality. What flashy or exciting experiences do you wish your Christian life had more of?

6. Suppose you invited your non-Christian neighbor to your church service. What might be strange or confusing to your friend?

7. What are you doing to build yourself up spiritually? What are you doing to build up your church?

CARING TIME

(Choose 1 or 2 of these questions before closing in prayer. Be sure to pray for the empty chair.)

1. What "revelation or knowledge or prophecy or word of instruction" (v. 6) has someone in this group shared that has helped you?

2. What is something you did for someone else this past week? What can you do this week?

3. How can the group remember you in prayer this week?

words to instruct others than ten thousand words in a tongue.

²⁰Brothers, stop thinking like children. In regard to evil be infants, but in your thinking be adults. ²¹In the Law it is written:

> "Through men of strange tongues
> > and through the lips of foreigners
> I will speak to this people,
> > but even then they will not listen to me,"^e

says the Lord.

²²Tongues, then, are a sign, not for believers but for unbelievers; prophecy, however, is for believers, not for unbelievers. ²³So if the whole church comes together and everyone speaks in tongues, and some who do not understand^f or some unbelievers come in, will they not say that you are out of your mind? ²⁴But if an unbeliever or someone who does not understand^g comes in while everybody is prophesying, he will be convinced by all that he is a sinner and will be judged by all, ²⁵and the secrets of his heart will be laid bare. So he will fall down and worship God, exclaiming, "God is really among you!"

---

[a]2 Or *another language;* also in verses 4,13,14,19,26 and 27   [b]2 Or *by the Spirit*
[c]5 Or *other languages;* also in verses 6,18,22,23 and 39   [d]16 Or *among the inquirers*
[e]21 Isaiah 28:11,12   [f]23 Or *some inquirers*   [g]24 Or *or some inquirer*

Summary. Paul attacks head-on the problem they are experiencing with the gift of tongues: during their worship services, far too much time was spent speaking in tongues. The result was that chaos, not order, prevailed. No one was edified, because no one knew what was going on! In these verses, Paul contrasts gifts that are intelligible and which edify the community (such as prophecy) with gifts that are unintelligible and which edify only the individual (such as tongues).

14:1 Paul defines the theme of chapter 14 by means of three propositions—imperatives that are to be followed in this order: First, "follow the way of love"; second, in that context, "eagerly desire spiritual gifts"; and third, in your eager desire for gifts which has love as its aim, "especially (desire) the gift of prophecy." The Corinthians had precisely the opposite order in their seeking *the* spiritual gift rather than gifts. And their aim was not love but being "spiritual" (Fee).

follow. In fact, the word might better be translated "pursue." It is virtually synonymous with the next verb: "eagerly desire."

the way of love. As defined in chapter 13, the "way of love" is the primary calling for all Christians and the context within which spiritual gifts are to be used.

eagerly desire. In 1 Corinthians 12:31 Paul told the Corinthians to "eagerly desire" the greater gifts. By the reuse of the phrase here he connects chapter 14 back to chapter 12.

14:2–5 By using a series of contrasts, Paul shows why prophecy is to be preferred over tongues.

14:2 Paul's first point about tongues is that, while they may be intelligible to God (who, after all, is the source of tongues), they are not intelligible to other people.

14:3 In contrast, prophecy is intelligible and brings three benefits to the congregation: it builds them up, it encourages, and it comforts.

prophesies. This is not so much future prediction as it is moral exhortation and theological instruction—probably as related to particular problems and issues being faced by the community.

14:4 In the second contrast, Paul points out who is edified by each gift: while tongues edify the individual (and there is no hint that this is not of great value), prophecy edifies many (and the way of love would therefore give this gift primary emphasis).

14:5 While affirming the value of both tongues and prophecy, Paul stresses prophecy because of its value during the worship service.

tongues. In verses 2–5, Paul gives insight into just what tongues are. They seem to be a gift from the Holy Spirit whereby an individual "utters mysteries" to God by (or in) the Spirit, from which great personal benefit is gained. Uninterpreted tongues, however, are meant to be part of private devotions, not public worship.

greater. In the sense that prophecy edifies, and is therefore an act of love. Interpreted tongues have the same use and value as prophecy.

14:6–12 Now the real issue comes out: intelligibility (v. 9). It appears that it is not just prophecy that Paul is commending (v. 6). Prophecy is just the example he has chosen of an intelligible gift. Here, Paul examines the value of various gifts from the point of view of the other people in church.

14:6 *revelation / knowledge / prophecy / word of instruction.* These four gifts all deal with forms of Christian instruction. It is difficult to distinguish sharply between them. The differences may be in the content of the instruction: revelation dealing with hidden aspects of God's truth (Rom. 16:25; 2 Cor. 12:1,7); knowledge as exposition of revealed truth; prophecy as insight from God into a specific situation; and a word of instruction (literally, "teaching") as the general application of Christian truth.

14:7–11 Three illustrations show the importance of intelligibility in worship: musical instruments (v. 7), military trumpets (v. 8), and language (vv. 10–11).

14:7 The point of playing an instrument is not just to make sounds, but to play a recognizable tune.

14:8 A trumpet can be used to alert an army for battle, but if the wrong note (or a weak note) is sounded, the soldiers will be unclear as to what is expected of them. It will be merely noise to them.

14:9 *speaking into the air.* This is what tongues are from the standpoint of the hearer—mere random sound.

14:10–11 While each language has meaning (tongues presumably have meaning to God), when spoken to a foreigner, this language is just gibberish—the one speaking might as well have said absolutely nothing.

14:11 *foreigner.* The Greek word is *barbaros* (barbarian). Foreigners were so named because to cultured Greek ears, their languages sounded like gibberish, as if they were saying, "brrbrr."

14:12 In summing up his argument, Paul commends their desire for spiritual gifts, but urges them to seek those that build up others.

14:13–25 Paul focuses on the use of tongues in public worship.

14:13 Those with the gift of tongues should pray for the ability to interpret so that the gift can be useful for others.

For this reason. Because intelligible gifts edify, Paul next shows how tongues might become such.

14:14–17 Paul explains how he understands tongues.

14:14 *my spirit.* The work of the Holy Spirit in each Christian is expressed via spiritual gifts—in this case, the gift of tongues is in view. In the Spirit, Paul both prays and sings in tongues, as well as in normal language (in his case, Greek).

14:15 *pray with my spirit.* Paul adds another insight into tongues: this is prayer that bypasses the mind. It is, according to verse 15, one quite legitimate (and edifying—v. 4) means of prayer, but it is meant to be complemented with prayer that engages the mind.

14:16 *those who do not understand.* Switching back to the public context, Paul notes that since inquirers coming to a worship service would not understand tongues, they are therefore inappropriate in that context (see vv. 23–24).

Amen. If a person does not understand what is being said in prayer, it is not possible to share in it and offer this traditional response of affirmation used in th Jewish and Christian services.

14:18–19 Paul picks up his argument again, and reasserts his view that while tongues are indeed a gift from God ("I thank God that I speak in tongues"), intelligible gifts are to be used in church.

14:20–25 Paul has made the point that tongues are not capable of edifying the church during worship. Here he challenges them to rethink their understanding of the function of tongues (v. 20); he illustrates his point with an Old Testament text (v. 21); and then makes his application by means of two assertions and two illustrations (vv. 22–25).

14:20 They are like children fascinated by that which is novel and exciting rather than like adults who can discern that which has value (13:11). While he wants them to be as innocent as children regarding evil, he wants them to think reasonably like adults so they will stop emphasizing a gift that has limited use in the edification of the church.

14:21 Paul points to the Old Testament to demonstrate that people will not respond (in repentance and faith) to strange tongues. "Paul goes back to Isaiah 28:9–12. ... Isaiah has preached to [the people of God] in their own Hebrew language and they have not listened and understood. Because of their disobedience the Assyrians will come upon them and will conquer them and will occupy their cities and then they will have to listen to language which they cannot understand. They will have to listen to the foreign tongues of their conquerors speaking unintelligible things; and not even that terrible experience will make an unbelieving people turn to God" (Barclay).

the Law. Strictly speaking the Law referred to the first five books of our Old Testament; but by extension, it referred to the whole Old Testament.

> *Prophecy, the revelation of God's truth in normal language, is for the good of those who believe.*

14:22 *Tongues, then, are a sign.* This is a difficult verse. Paul seems to mean that tongues are a sign of *judgment* against the unbeliever. This is compatible with the Isaiah text he has just quoted.

prophecy. Prophecy, the revelation of God's truth in normal language, is for the good of those who believe (or are honestly inquiring—v. 24). The Corinthians, however, seem to have closed their ears to difficult issues that may have been pointed out via prophecy, and preferred the unintelligibility of tongues.

14:23–25 Paul shifts back to his original line of reasoning, but now he contrasts the negative impact of tongues on unbelievers with the positive impact of prophecy on them. Prior to this, Paul has been concerned about the impact of tongues and prophecy on believers.

14:23 *everyone speaks in tongues.* The Corinthian worship service must have been a cacophony of noise and confusion, with the simultaneous exercise of tongues.

out of your mind. Not in the modern sense of "insane," but in the ancient sense of "possessed by a spirit."

14:24 *while everybody is prophesying.* "This passage … implies that prophesying is potentially available to all believers since all are Spirit people. That is, Paul does not say, 'If the prophets all prophesy …,' but, 'If all prophesy … the unbeliever will be convicted by all … and he will be judged by all.' The nature of this argumentation seems to exclude the option that this gift was limited to a group of authoritative people who were known in the community as 'the prophets' " (Fee).

14:25 Prophecy invokes conviction and commitment; tongues invoke nothing more than a cognitive sense that the speaker is possessed in the same way as devotees from other religions.

fall down. This is to acknowledge one's own unworthiness before God.

Comment: "God is really among you!"

Paul ends this section by discussing the impact of tongues and prophecy on *unbelievers*. In verse 23 he points out that were an unbeliever to come into a worship service at Corinth and find all the believers speaking in tongues, that person would be baffled. Although it would be assumed that a "god" had come upon the people (since this type of ecstatic speech was part of certain temple rituals), no one would know anything else. The name of Christ, much less the Gospel story, would not have been preached. Therefore, no response to Jesus on the part of the unbeliever would be possible.

However, if prophecy occurred, since everyone could understand what was being said, it would become evident to the unbeliever that the true God was indeed dwelling in this place. This individual would be amazed and moved by the depth and meaning of the prophecy, and would be convicted by the Holy Spirit.

This is what people are looking for today—desperately. If God is alive and real they want to know him. The exercise of the intelligible gifts is often a clear sign to people that God is alive. Such gifts still bring conviction of heart even day as they did 2,000 years ago.

THREE-PART AGENDA

ICE-BREAKER	**BIBLE STUDY**	**CARING TIME**
15 Minutes	30 Minutes	15–45 Minutes

> **LEADER: How is the process going of identifying an Apprentice / Leader to start a new small group (see page M6 in the center section)? Check the list of ice-breakers on page M7, especially if you have a new person in this session.**

TO BEGIN THE BIBLE STUDY TIME
(Choose 1 or 2)

1. What is one of your favorite hymns or Christian choruses?

2. What church did you attend as a child? How regularly? What was it like?

3. What was the most inspiring part of a worship service you've attended recently: The music? The sermon? A prayer? Communion? A testimony? A greeting from someone? Other?

READ SCRIPTURE & DISCUSS
(If you don't have time for all the questions in this section, conclude the Bible Study [30 min.] by answering question #7.)

1. How would you describe the style of worship at your church: Traditional? Contemporary? Quiet? Orderly? Noisy? Balanced? Other?

2. What was wrong with the Corinthian style of worship? What guidelines for worship do we find in this passage?

3. In what ways does your worship experience parallel what Paul says in verse 26? How does it differ?

Orderly Worship

26 What then shall we say, brothers? When you come together, everyone has a hymn, or a word of instruction, a revelation, a tongue or an interpretation. All of these must be done for the strengthening of the church. 27 If anyone speaks in a tongue, two—or at the most three—should speak, one at a time, and someone must interpret. 28 If there is no interpreter, the speaker should keep quiet in the church and speak to himself and God.

29 Two or three prophets should speak, and the others should weigh carefully what is said. 30 And if a revelation comes to someone who is sitting down, the first speaker should stop. 31 For you can all prophesy in turn so that everyone may be instructed and encouraged. 32 The spirits of prophets are subject to the control of prophets. 33 For God is not a God of disorder but of peace.

As in all the congregations of the saints, 34 women should remain silent in the churches. They are not allowed to speak, but must be in submission, as the Law says. 35 If they want to inquire about something, they should ask their own husbands at home; for it is disgraceful for a woman to speak in the church.

36 Did the word of God originate with you? Or are you the only people it has reached? 37 If anybody thinks he is a prophet or spiritually gifted, let him acknowledge that what I am writing to you is the Lord's command. 38 If he ignores this, he himself will be ignored. [a]

39 Therefore, my brothers, be eager to prophesy, and do not forbid speaking in tongues. 40 But everything should be done in a fitting and orderly way.

---

[a] 38 Some manuscripts *If he is ignorant of this, let him be ignorant*

4. How do you feel about the use of the gifts of tongues and interpretation and prophecy today? By what standards should Christians "weigh carefully what is said" (v. 29)?

5. Verse 33 says, "God is not a God of disorder but of peace." What does this characteristic of God mean to you?

6. Verses 34–35 are quite difficult to understand (see notes). What type of talk, contributing to general disorder, might be in view here?

7. What can you do to improve the quality of your worship experience?

CARING TIME

(Choose 1 or 2 of these questions before closing in prayer. Be sure to pray for the empty chair.)

1. What has been the "tone" of worship in your spiritual life this week: Ecstatic and loud? Quiet and reverent? Somber? Other?

2. What challenge are you facing this week or in the near future?

3. How would you like the group to pray for you this week?

Notes—1 Corinthians 14:26–40

Summary. Paul concludes this major section (begun in 11:2) by outlining quite specifically how certain spiritual gifts are to be used when the church assembles together—his main point being that when it comes to worship, order—not disorder—is the way of God.

14:26 Paul reiterates that each believer has a gift to offer during worship, that there are a variety of gifts, and that gifts are to be used to edify.

a hymn. Singing is a gift. The reference here may be to "singing in the Spirit" (14:15).

All of these. Probably a representative list of the sort of gifts used during worship. The list is not exhaustive because it does not include, for example, prophecy or discernment of spirits (previously mentioned in the context of worship, and assumed in the verses that follow).

14:27–28 Paul offers guidelines for the use of tongues: only two or three are to speak, one at a time, and never (in church) without interpretation.

14:29–33 Here he gives guidelines for prophecy: two or three speak, followed by discernment.

14:29 ***weigh carefully.*** Simply because a prophecy is uttered does not make it automatically true. Not only does its "source" have to be noted by those gifted in such discernment (12:10), but its content must be considered carefully by the whole body (12:3; 1 Thess. 5:20–21).

14:30 ***a revelation.*** This might be some type of pressing vision, the content of which must be shared right away before it passes.

14:31–32 These "seem to be directives against those who would tend to dominate and talk too long" (Fee).

14:31 While it is true that certain individuals held the office of prophet (and had a special, recognized gift of prophecy—Acts 11:27–28; 21:9–11), here Paul says that on occasion anyone might exercise the gift of prophecy.

14:32 In fact, prophets can control their utterances. A prophet (or tongues-speaker—14:15) is not gripped by such a frenzy that "automatic speaking" results, which bypasses the control of the person. Thus, order is possible within the assembly.

14:33b ***As in all the congregations of the saints.*** It can be argued that the last half of verse 33 belongs not with verse 34 (as the NIV has it), but with the first half of verse 33. (The NIV phrase "in all the congregations" is followed awkwardly by the parallel phrase in v. 34, "in the churches.") In other words, Paul is saying that God is the God of peace in all congregations. Hence their worship likewise should reflect peace.

14:34–35 These are very difficult verses to interpret since they seem to contradict chapter 11 (especially 11:5), where Paul indicates that as long as women are suitably clothed they can pray and prophesy during public worship. A variety of solutions have been proposed: (1) that verses 34–35 were a later addition to the text, not by Paul (v. 33 flows smoothly into v. 36); (2) that what Paul prohibits is women passing judgment on prophecy as in verse 29; (3) that the reference is to uninspired "chatter" (the word means this in classical Greek) by the women which is adding to the chaos. Rather than clamoring for explanations during worship, women should raise questions with their husbands when they get home (v. 35). Obviously Paul understood how verses 34–35 correlated with 11:2–16, since he would not have written contradictory advice. The problem is that no one today knows for sure what is meant.

14:36 Now Paul concludes by directly confronting the Corinthians over the fact that they considered tongues to be what made one "spiritual." In this matter, they cannot assume that they alone know the truth, nor that God gave only them this insight.

14:37–38 As to those who are teaching this, if they are really inspired by the Holy Spirit (as Paul indeed knows that he is—2:16; 7:40), they cannot help but agree. The Spirit does not inspire opposing messages.

14:39–40 Paul summarizes chapter 14 with three commands—the first two relate to verses 1–25, and the third to verses 26–35.

Comment: Tongues and Interpretation
by C. Peter Wagner

The gift of tongues is the special ability that God gives to certain members of the Body of Christ (A) to speak to God in a language they have never learned and/or (B) to receive and communicate an immediate message of God to His people through a divinely-anointed utterance in a language they have never learned. ...

Private tongues are often referred to as "prayer language." No accompanying gift of interpretation is involved. The biblical text most descriptive of this is 1 Corinthians 14:28 where Paul says that tongues without interpretation should not be used in the church, but rather the person who has such a gift should "speak to himself, and to God." ...

This function has been described by Harald Bredesen ... in several postulates:

1. "Tongues enable our spirits to communicate directly with God above and beyond the power of our minds to understand."

2. "Tongues liberate the Spirit of God within us."

3. "Tongues enable the spirit to take its place of ascendancy over soul and body."

4. "Tongues are God's provision for catharsis, therefore important to our mental health."

5. "Tongues meet our needs for a whole new language for worship, prayer and praise." ...

Part B or public tongues is intimately related to the gift of interpretation. Without interpretation the gift is useless and has no part in the church (see 1 Cor. 14:27,28).

The gift of interpretation is the special ability that God gives to certain members of the Body of Christ to make known in the vernacular the message of one who speaks in tongues.

Quite often, but not always, tongues-interpretation functions as a hyphenated gift. Michael Green says, "Though some men have the gift of interpretation who cannot themselves speak in tongues, this is unusual; for the most part it is those who already have tongues who gain this further gift of interpretation." This means that some people give messages in public in tongues and immediately interpret what they themselves have said. In other cases one will give the message and another will interpret. ...

By way of example I will relate a secondhand anecdote that I received from a very reliable source. It involves a group of believers in a remote Guatemalan village. A severe drought had devastated the area and the village was on the verge of extinction. The Christians prayed and God spoke to the group through a message in tongues. He told them to go up on a hill which was owned by the Christians and dig a well. It seemed to be one of the most illogical places to do it, but they obeyed, even in the face of the ridicule of the unbelievers in the village. The ridicule changed to astonishment, however, when they soon struck an abundant supply of water and the entire village was saved. Many unbelievers also were saved when they saw the power of God. Maybe this is what Paul had in mind when he wrote, "Tongues are for a sign, not to them that believe, but to them that believe not" (1 Cor. 14:22).

Taken from *Your Spiritual Gifts Can Help Your Church Grow* (Regal Books, 1979), pp. 233–236.

20 Christ Arose—1 Cor. 15:1–11

THREE-PART AGENDA

ICE-BREAKER
15 Minutes

BIBLE STUDY
30 Minutes

CARING TIME
15–45 Minutes

> *LEADER: To help you identify people who might form the core of a new small group (or if a new person comes to this meeting), see the listing of ice-breakers on page M7 of the center section.*

TO BEGIN THE BIBLE STUDY TIME
(Choose 1 or 2)

1. What great or "historic" event have you witnessed?

2. What are your favorite memories of celebrating Easter?

3. What piece of advice were you given as a child that you have never forgotten?

READ SCRIPTURE & DISCUSS
(If you don't have time for all the questions in this section, conclude the Bible Study [30 min.] by answering question #7.)

1. Who in your life has been there to help keep you on "the straight and narrow"?

2. In reminding the Corinthians about the Gospel, Paul describes it as "on which you have taken your stand." How had the Corinthians "taken their stand" on the Gospel?

3. What are the main points of the Gospel Paul received and passed on to the Corinthians?

4. How important is it to your faith that Jesus rose from the dead? How would you explain the importance of Christ's resurrection to a non-Christian?

The Resurrection of Christ

15 *Now, brothers, I want to remind you of the gospel I preached to you, which you received and on which you have taken your stand. ²By this gospel you are saved, if you hold firmly to the word I preached to you. Otherwise, you have believed in vain.*

³For what I received I passed on to you as of first importance[a]*: that Christ died for our sins according to the Scriptures, ⁴that he was buried, that he was raised on the third day according to the Scriptures, ⁵and that he appeared to Peter,*[b] *and then to the Twelve. ⁶After that, he appeared to more than five hundred of the brothers at the same time, most of whom are still living, though some have fallen asleep. ⁷Then he appeared to James, then to all the apostles, ⁸and last of all he appeared to me also, as to one abnormally born.*

⁹For I am the least of the apostles and do not even deserve to be called an apostle, because I persecuted the church of God. ¹⁰But by the grace of God I am what I am, and his grace to me was not without effect. No, I worked harder than all of them—yet not I, but the grace of God that was with me. ¹¹Whether, then, it was I or they, this is what we preach, and this is what you believed.

[a]3 Or *you at the first*   [b]5 Greek *Cephas*

5. Why do you think Paul went to such detail listing who saw Jesus after he was resurrected?

6. Why does Paul refer to himself in verse 8 as having been one "abnormally born"?

7. What does "Christ died for our sins" (v. 3) mean to you? In what way has God's grace had effect in your life?

CARING TIME

(Choose 1 or 2 of these questions before closing in prayer.)

1. How has God been at work in your life this past week?

2. What concern do you have about this week or the near future?

3. How can the group pray for you in the coming week?

Notes—1 Corinthians 15:1–11

Summary. In chapter 15 Paul turns to a theological problem, in contrast to the largely behavioral problems he has dealt with thus far. Some Corinthians are denying that in the future believers will be raised from the dead. The problem may be simply one of ignorance. No one instructed them in this matter. (The Thessalonians, for example, did not know about the resurrection of the dead, as Paul says in 1 Thess. 4:13–18.) Furthermore, the Corinthians might have resisted this concept, since it ran counter to the Gnostic idea that death released the spirit to return to God, and the useless body (in the Gnostic view) fell away like a discarded husk. Or, like Hymenaeus and Philetus, they might have "spiritualized" the resurrection, saying that it has already taken place (2 Tim. 2:17–18).

15:1–11 Paul begins this chapter by pointing to something the Corinthians believed: that Christ rose from the dead. Christ's resurrection is the key to Paul's argument that believers will also be resurrected.

15:1 *gospel.* Literally, "good news"; a term used in Greek literature to signify a positive event of great significance (for example, the birth of a future emperor or the winning of an important battle). It is used by Paul (and others in the New Testament) to designate the core message of Christianity—that in Jesus Christ God fulfilled his promises and opened a way of salvation to all people. In the next few verses, Paul will define the content of this message.

15:2 It is as a result of belief (trust) in the Good News of Christ's death and resurrection that salvation comes.

15:3–4 This is the earliest written definition of the "Gospel." It consists of three statements of historical fact (Christ died, was buried, and rose again), and two words of explanation—he died "for our sins" (i.e., to deal with them), and all this is "according to the Scriptures" (i.e., a fulfillment of God's plan).

15:3 *what I received.* Paul did not make up the Gospel. It was common to the church. He simply passed on what he had been given.

for our sins. When Christ died, it was in order to deal with the fact of our sin. By his death as a substitute in our place, Christ enabled men and women to be forgiven for their sins, to come back into relationship with God, and to have new life.

according to the Scriptures. Christ's death fulfilled the prophecies found in Old Testament Scripture (e.g., Isaiah 52:13–53:12). "This means that it was not fortuitous, but willed and determined by God, and that it formed part of the winding up of his eternal purpose; that is, that it was one of those eschatological events that stand on the frontier between the present age and the age to come, in which the divine purpose reaches its completion" (Barrett).

15:4 *he was buried.* Jesus was really dead, and so he really rose from the dead. It was a real resurrection, not just resuscitation.

he was raised. Paul shifts the tense of the verb (in Greek) from the aorist tense (completed past action—"died / buried") to the perfect tense, with the idea that what once happened is even now still in force. "Christ died, but he is not dead; he was buried, but he is not in the grave; he was raised, and he is alive now" (Barrett).

> When Christ died, it was in order to deal with the fact of our sin. By his death as a substitute in our place, Christ enabled men and women to be forgiven for their sins, to come back into relationship with God, and to have new life.

15:5 *he appeared.* Paul's emphasis in this statement of the Gospel is on Jesus' resurrection (because of the argument he is building in chapter 15), so here he points to six post-resurrection appearances, each of which substantiate that Christ indeed rose.

to Peter. Mark 16:7 and Luke 24:34.

to the Twelve. Matthew 28:16–20; Luke 24:31–51; John 20:19–23.

15:6 *to more than five hundred ... most of whom are still living.* Paul is inviting people to check out for themselves the reality of Christ's resurrection. What he is saying is: "There are more than 500 people who some 20 years ago saw Jesus after his resurrection. Ask one of them." This is a strong proof of Christ's resurrection, because in this public letter Paul would never have challenged people in this way if these witnesses had not, indeed, seen the resurrected Christ and could therefore be counted upon to verify this fact.

15:7 *to James.* This appearance is not recorded, but James was widely respected as the leader of the church in Jerusalem.

to all the apostles. For example, in Acts 1:6–11.

15:8 *last of all ... to me.* This appearance came several years after the resurrection of Christ (Acts 9:1–8).

abnormally born. This probably refers to the fact that, unlike Peter and James, circumstances were such that Paul never knew Jesus during his earthly ministry.

15:9–11 For the third time (chapters 1–4, chapter 9), Paul defends his apostleship. Having used his own experience of the resurrected Lord as one of his six examples, it is quite natural to use it also to demonstrate the fact of his apostleship.

15:11 Paul reiterates that the Gospel he has just described is common to the church, preached by all, and believed by the Corinthians.

Comment: The Significance of the Resurrection
by John R.W. Stott

Clearly the resurrection has great significance. If it can be shown that Jesus of Nazareth rose from the dead, it is beyond dispute that he was a unique figure. It is not a question of his spiritual survival, nor of his physical resuscitation, but of his conquest of death and his resurrection to a new plane of existence altogether. We do not know of anyone else who has had this experience. ...

We may not feel that His resurrection establishes His deity conclusively, but we must agree that it is suggestive of it. It is fitting that a supernatural person should enter and leave the earth in a supernatural way. This is in fact what the New Testament teaches and the Church believes. His birth was natural, but His conception was supernatural. His death was natural, but His resurrection was supernatural. His miraculous conception and resurrection do not prove his deity, but they are congruous with it. We are not concerned here with his so-called "Virgin Birth." There is good reason to believe it, but it is not used in the New Testament to prove him Messiah and Son of God, as is the resurrection. Jesus himself never predicted his passion without adding that he would rise, and described his coming resurrection as a "sign." St. Paul, at the beginning of his Epistle to the Romans, writes that Jesus was "designated Son of God in power ... by his resurrection from the dead" (1:4), and the earliest sermons of the apostles recorded in the Acts repeatedly assert that by the resurrection God has reversed man's sentence and vindicated his Son.

Of this resurrection St. Luke, who is known to have been an accurate and painstaking historian, says there are "many infallible proofs" (Acts 1:3). We may not feel able to go as far as Matthew Arnold who called the resurrection "the best attested fact in history," but certainly many impartial students have judged the evidence to be extremely good. For instance, Sir Edward Clark, K.C., wrote to the Rev. E.L. Macassey, D.D.: "As a lawyer I have made a prolonged study of the evidences for the events of the first Easter Day. To me the evidence is conclusive, and over and over again in the High Court I have secured the verdict on evidence not nearly so compelling. Inference follows on evidence, and a truthful witness is always artless and disdains effect. The Gospel evidence for the resurrection is of this class, and as a lawyer I accept it unreservedly as the testimony of truthful men to facts they were able to substantiate."—*Basic Christianity* (Grand Rapids, MI: Wm. B. Eerdmans, 1958), pp. 45–46.

THREE-PART AGENDA

ICE-BREAKER	BIBLE STUDY	CARING TIME
15 Minutes	30 Minutes	15–45 Minutes

> **LEADER: Has your group discussed its plans on what to study after this course is finished? What about the mission project described on page M6 in the center section?**

TO BEGIN THE BIBLE STUDY TIME
(Choose 1 or 2)

1. What was the first funeral you can remember going to? What effect did it have on you?

2. When you were a child, what friend or other person was a bad influence on you?

3. When in your life have you had the attitude "eat, drink and be merry"?

READ SCRIPTURE & DISCUSS
(If you don't have time for all the questions in this section, conclude the Bible Study [30 min.] by answering question #7.)

1. How prevalent today is the philosophy Paul quotes in verse 32: "Let us eat and drink, for tomorrow we die"? Give an example.

2. What false teaching was being spread among the Corinthians (v. 12)?

3. From this passage, what does Paul say would be true if there were no resurrection of the dead?

The Resurrection of the Dead

¹²But if it is preached that Christ has been raised from the dead, how can some of you say that there is no resurrection of the dead? ¹³If there is no resurrection of the dead, then not even Christ has been raised. ¹⁴And if Christ has not been raised, our preaching is useless and so is your faith. ¹⁵More than that, we are then found to be false witnesses about God, for we have testified about God that he raised Christ from the dead. But he did not raise him if in fact the dead are not raised. ¹⁶For if the dead are not raised, then Christ has not been raised either. ¹⁷And if Christ has not been raised, your faith is futile; you are still in your sins. ¹⁸Then those also who have fallen asleep in Christ are lost. ¹⁹If only for this life we have hope in Christ, we are to be pitied more than all men.

²⁰But Christ has indeed been raised from the dead, the firstfruits of those who have fallen asleep. ²¹For since death came through a man, the resurrection of the dead comes also through a man. ²²For as in Adam all die, so in Christ all will be made alive. ²³But each in his own turn: Christ, the firstfruits; then, when he comes, those who belong to him. ²⁴Then the end will come, when he hands over the kingdom to God the Father after he has destroyed all dominion, authority and power. ²⁵For he must reign until he has put all his enemies under his feet. ²⁶The last enemy to be destroyed is death. ²⁷For he "has put everything under his feet."ᵃ Now when it says that "everything" has been put under him, it is clear that this does not include God himself, who put everything under Christ. ²⁸When he has done this, then the Son himself will be made subject to him who put everything under him, so that God may be all in all.

²⁹Now if there is no resurrection, what will those do who are baptized for the dead? If the dead are not raised at all, why are people baptized for them? ³⁰And as for us, why do we endanger ourselves every hour? ³¹I die every day—I mean that, brothers—just as surely as I glory over you in Christ Jesus our Lord. ³²If I fought wild beasts in Ephesus for merely human reasons, what have I gained? If the dead are not raised,

4. How can too close of an association with "bad company" (v. 33) affect your faith? When have you gotten too wrapped up with bad influences to the detriment of your faith?

5. When have you felt that life was futile and without hope?

6. How does the future resurrection bring hope and purpose to your life? How would your life be different without your hope that you will be resurrected?

7. How can you demonstrate the hope you have in Christ this coming week?

CARING TIME
(Choose 1 or 2 of these questions before closing in prayer.)

1. Who would you choose as the leader if this group "gave birth" to a new small group? Who else would you choose to be part of the leadership core for a new group?

2. How are you doing at spending personal time in prayer and Bible study?

3. In what specific way can this group pray for you this week?

> *"Let us eat and drink,*
>   *for tomorrow we die."*[b]
>
> [33]*Do not be misled: "Bad company corrupts good charac-*
> *ter." [34]Come back to your senses as you ought, and stop*
> *sinning; for there are some who are ignorant of God—I say*
> *this to your shame.*

[a]27 Psalm 8:6   [b]32 Isaiah 22:13

Notes—1 Corinthians 15:12–34

Summary. By means of a series of "if ... then" arguments, Paul shows that to deny the future resurrection of believers one must also deny the past resurrection of Jesus, which in fact the Corinthians apparently did not deny.

15:12 *But.* Having established the fact of Christ's resurrection (15:3–8), Paul now pushes the argument forward: Jesus' resurrection is a clear proof that there is such a thing as resurrection.

how can some of you say. Now Paul pinpoints directly the false teaching against which he is contending.

15:13–15 In the next if/then argument, Paul shows that if resurrection is impossible, then: (a) Christ could not have been raised, (b) Paul's own preaching is without value, (c) their faith is meaningless, and (d) they are lying about God.

15:14 *our preaching / your faith.* The Corinthians owe their very existence as a church to these two things: Paul's preaching and their response of faith. Central to both the preaching and their faith is the resurrection of Christ. And since the church does indeed exist, this is another proof of Christ's resurrection.

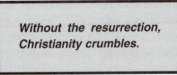

Without the resurrection, Christianity crumbles.

15:16 *if the dead are not raised.* This is the first of three times in this section (vv. 12–34) that Paul uses this phrase which summarizes the implications of their errant view about the resurrection of the body. If the dead are not raised, then: (a) Christ could not have been resurrected (and they believe that he was), (b) there would be no point in baptizing people for the dead (as they were apparently doing—v. 29), and (c) believers might as well "live it up," since they had no future (v. 32).

15:17–19 Relentlessly, Paul points out to his readers the implications of no resurrection: (a) they are still lost and dead in sin, (b) those who have died are lost, (c) their "hope" is groundless, and (d) they are pitiable people. Without the resurrection, Christianity crumbles.

15:20–28 The future resurrection of believers is the logical outcome of Christ's past resurrection.

15:20 *But Christ has indeed been raised.* Having sketched the horror of no resurrection, Paul relieves the gloom and shifts to this positive affirmation. This is the essential declaration, without which there is no Christianity.

100

firstfruits. The early developing grains or fruits that demonstrate that the full harvest is not far behind. Similarly, the fact that Christ was raised from the dead is clear proof that the future resurrection of believers is assured.

15:21–22 From the metaphor of the firstfruits, Paul moves to the analogy of Christ and Adam. It is via Adam that all died. It is via Christ that death is undone. Paul will treat this metaphor in more detail in 15:45–49.

15:22 *Adam.* Adam sinned, and so death entered into the world (Gen. 2:17); and thus all people since that time experience death (Rom. 5:12–21).

all will be made alive. Though the wording has been made parallel to the previous clause ("all die"), the idea is that all who are *in Christ* will rise, as Paul says explicitly in 1 Thessalonians 4:16.

15:23–28 Paul returns to the metaphor of the firstfruits, showing how it relates to the Second Coming. In order for the Corinthians to understand the future resurrection, Paul must place it in the context of the time when Christ returns.

15:23 Christ was raised on the third day after his death (15:4). Christians will be raised at his second coming.

15:24–26 After Christ has defeated the powers of evil, he will hand over the kingdom to God—the key event of the end times (see Psalm 110:1).

15:26 The last of these enemies to be rendered impotent (inoperative) is death itself. That Christ has won out is seen in the resurrection of believers.

15:27–28 Paul quotes and explains Psalm 8:6 as the basis for what he has said.

15:29–34 Thus far, Paul has shown that there is a resurrection for believers in the future. In this section, he points out that both his actions and theirs demonstrate a belief in the resurrection of the dead.

15:29 *if there is no resurrection.* Here Paul gives the first of three arguments which point out the absurdity of an action if there is no coming resurrection. In verse 29, the absurd action is baptism for the dead.

baptized for the dead. It seems that among the strange things that happened at Corinth was the practice (by some) of vicarious baptism. A living person was immersed in water on behalf of a dead person to secure, as if by magic, the benefits of baptism for the departed friend. At least this is the best guess of scholars as to what was going on. Paul refers to this ritual as part of his argument for the resurrection of the dead without necessarily endorsing its practice.

15:30–32a Next, Paul argues that it is absurd for him to undergo the dangers he does for the sake of Christianity if there is no hope of resurrection.

15:32 *fought wild beasts.* Paul may be speaking metaphorically, or he may be referring to persecution he suffered in Ephesus involving fighting wild animals for the entertainment of others (similar to what went on in the Coliseum in Rome at a later time). Paul could also be referring to wild animals he fought as he traveled throughout Asia Minor preaching the Gospel.

> *After Christ has defeated the power of evil, he will hand over the kingdom to God—the key event of the end times.*

15:32b–34 The third appeal goes like this: If there is no resurrection, then there is nothing in the future for a person; therefore, life has no purpose beyond the here-and-now—so live it up!

15:33 *"Bad company corrupts good character."* This is a quote taken from the comedy *Thais*, written by Menander. It had become a well-known proverb by Paul's time. Paul generally quoted from the Old Testament, so this quotation from a secular source is an unusual departure for him. Paul's point here is that those who are teaching that there is no resurrection (v. 12) are corrupting those who adhere to the true doctrine.

15:34 *stop sinning.* Perhaps this reveals why Paul wrote this section of the letter. The Corinthians may have used their denial of the resurrection of the body to justify their involvement in indulgence and immorality (1 Cor. 6:12ff).

THREE-PART AGENDA

ICE-BREAKER
15 Minutes

BIBLE STUDY
30 Minutes

CARING TIME
15–45 Minutes

> *LEADER: Has your group finalized its plans on what to study after this course is finished? What about the mission project described on page M6 in the center section?*

TO BEGIN THE BIBLE STUDY TIME
(Choose 1 or 2)

1. What would you like to change about your body?

2. When you get to heaven, who is the first person you are going to look up?

3. What's the closest you've ever been to death?

READ SCRIPTURE & DISCUSS
(If you don't have time for all the questions in this section, conclude the Bible Study [30 min.] by answering question #7.)

1. How do you feel about dying? What do you believe happens to a person when they die?

2. What practical concern undercut belief in the resurrection of the dead for some of the Corinthians (v. 35)?

3. What are the characteristics of the resurrection body that Christians will receive?

4. What is the sting of death? How did Jesus win the victory over death? How can you share in this victory?

5. What insights in this passage about the life to come are most striking to you? What excites you? What puzzles you?

The Resurrection Body

35But someone may ask, "How are the dead raised? With what kind of body will they come?" 36How foolish! What you sow does not come to life unless it dies. 37When you sow, you do not plant the body that will be, but just a seed, perhaps of wheat or of something else. 38But God gives it a body as he has determined, and to each kind of seed he gives its own body. 39All flesh is not the same: Men have one kind of flesh, animals have another, birds another and fish another. 40There are also heavenly bodies and there are earthly bodies; but the splendor of the heavenly bodies is one kind, and the splendor of the earthly bodies is another. 41The sun has one kind of splendor, the moon another and the stars another; and star differs from star in splendor.

42So will it be with the resurrection of the dead. The body that is sown is perishable, it is raised imperishable; 43it is sown in dishonor, it is raised in glory; it is sown in weakness, it is raised in power; 44it is sown a natural body, it is raised a spiritual body.

If there is a natural body, there is also a spiritual body. 45So it is written: "The first man Adam became a living being"; the last Adam, a life-giving spirit. 46The spiritual did not come first, but the natural, and after that the spiritual. 47The first man was of the dust of the earth, the second man from heaven. 48As was the earthly man, so are those who are of the earth; and as is the man from heaven, so also are those who are of heaven. 49And just as we have borne the likeness of the earthly man, so shall we bear the likeness of the man from heaven.

50I declare to you, brothers, that flesh and blood cannot inherit the kingdom of God, nor does the perishable inherit the imperishable. 51Listen, I tell you a mystery: We will not all sleep, but we will all be changed— 52in a flash, in the twinkling of an eye, at the last trumpet. For the trumpet will sound, the dead will be raised imperishable, and we will be changed. 53For the perishable must clothe itself with the imperishable, and the mortal with immortality. 54When the perishable has been clothed with the imperishable, and the mortal with immortality, then the saying that is written will come true: "Death has been swallowed up in victory."

6. What is most comforting to you from these verses when you consider the reality of your own eventual death?

7. What grade would you give yourself for this last week on being devoted "fully to the work of the Lord" (v. 58)? What can you do this week to improve your grade?

CARING TIME
(Answer all the questions below, then take prayer requests and close with prayer.)

1. Next week will be the last session in this study. How would you like to celebrate: A dinner? A party?

2. What is the next step for this group: Start a new group? Continue with another study?

3. What prayer needs or praises would you like to share?

(If the group plans to continue, see the back inside cover for what's available from Serendipity.)

> 55 *"Where, O death, is your victory?*
> *Where, O death, is your sting?"*
>
> 56 *The sting of death is sin, and the power of sin is the law.*
> 57 *But thanks be to God! He gives us the victory through our Lord Jesus Christ.*
>
> 58 *Therefore, my dear brothers, stand firm. Let nothing move you. Always give yourselves fully to the work of the Lord, because you know that your labor in the Lord is not in vain.*

Notes—1 Corinthians 15:35–58

Summary. The false teachers in Corinth may be arguing against the future resurrection by asserting that it is absurd to imagine "the resuscitation of an immense number of corpses" (Barrett). The question is "foolish" (v. 36) when put that way, especially since it misses the whole point of the resurrection, which is the transformation of the natural into the spiritual. Still, Paul must deal with the issue, and so the subject of verses 35–58 is the nature of the resurrection body.

15:35 This is the question the false teachers raise.

15:36–38 Death brings change (transformation), not extinction. Here, Paul probes the nature of the transformation; his point being that what one plants (or buries) is not what one gets in the end. A small grain of wheat grows mysteriously into a tall, grain-bearing stalk (John 12:24). So, too, their bodies will yield new and glorious bodies after the resurrection.

15:39–41 A second analogy is used to show that there are a host of different kinds of bodies, and it is not unreasonable to expect the resurrection body to be quite different from the natural body.

15:42–44a Paul reinforces the idea of verse 36: what is sown in one way is raised in another. He makes this point by means of a series of antithetical comparisons: perishable / imperishable; dishonor / glory; weakness / power; natural / spiritual.

15:42 *perishable.* Literally, "corruption." This "is an evil power, by which the world is dominated in the old age. ... It affects not only human life, but the whole of creation. Its dominion will be ended in the age to come, at the beginning of which the resurrection takes place. Thus Paul's point is not simply that we shall have a new body, no longer subject to change and decay; but that new body will be appropriate to the new age" (Barrett).

15:43 Paul now describes the nature of the changed body. The resurrection body is characterized by glory (brightness, radiance, splendor). This is a quality ascribed to God, in which believers will somehow share (Phil. 3:21). The resurrection body will also be filled with power—another word often used to describe Christ.

15:44 *natural / spiritual.* The natural body is that which is animated by the soul (i.e., the natural life force), while the spiritual body has as its animating force the Holy Spirit.

15:44b Here, he reinforces verses 38–41: different bodies are appropriate to different circumstances. While having continuity with the natural body (which is the seed from which it springs), the spiritual body will be quite new and, in fact, will bear the marks of Christ's nature (v. 43).

15:45–49 Paul explains further the analogy of Adam and Christ (15:21–22), his point being that just as humans share the likeness of Adam's mortal body (Paul quotes Gen. 2:7 in this regard), they will share the likeness of Christ's spiritual body.

15:48 The Christians, after their resurrection, will become a race of heavenly people.

15:49 *the man from heaven.* This is Jesus, whose image Christians will reflect both in terms of character and glory.

15:50–58 Paul concludes his argument for the resurrection of believers with a magnificent passage in which he points triumphantly to the future hope of the Christian.

15:50 *flesh and blood.* That is, living people cannot inherit the kingdom.

perishable. Nor can the unchanged dead inherit the kingdom. What Paul is saying is that at the Second Coming neither the living nor the dead can take part in the kingdom without being changed.

15:51 *mystery.* A truth about the end times, once hidden but now revealed.

We. Paul expected to be alive at the Second Coming.

not all sleep. Some Christians will be alive at the Second Coming.

all be changed. Both the living and the dead will be changed.

15:52 *in a flash.* This change will occur instantaneously.

the trumpet will sound. The sounding of the trumpet was used to rally an army for action. This image is used to describe God's calling his people together (1 Thess. 4:16).

the dead will be raised. Those who are in the grave at the Second Coming will be transformed, as will the living.

15:54 *the saying that is written will come true.* Paul cites two texts from the Old Testament—here

(the quote is from Isaiah 25:8) and in verse 55—which have yet to be fulfilled. "This is the only instance of his citing yet unfulfilled prophecy; but as always he cites the Old Testament in light of the death and resurrection of Jesus. So these two passages are in fact fulfilled in Christ; they simply have yet to be realized" (Fee).

15:55 Death has been swallowed up in the victory of the resurrection. Using Hosea 13:14, Paul "taunts" death.

15:56 *The sting of death is sin.* "Considered genetically, the relationship means that sin is the cause of death; here it is considered empirically. Taking death as a given fact, sin is what embitters it, not only psychologically, in that it breeds remorse, but also theologically, in that it makes clear that death is not merely a natural phenomenon, but a punishment, an evil that need not exist and would not exist if man were not in rebellion against his Creator" (Barrett).

the power of sin is the law. By this paul means that the Law of God has the unfortunate result of arousing sin within people. As he shows from his own example in Romans 7, the Law's command not to covet did not deliver him from covetousness but actually stirred him up to feel it all the more.

15:57 *victory.* In great joy, Paul exults in the fact that sin and the Law (that by which sin is made known) do not have the last word. Christ's death was a victory over sin and death.

15:58 *stand firm.* His letter is at an end; his chastening is finished, and so it is appropriate that he challenge them to allow this same Christ who has won victories for them to win victories through them.

your labor in the Lord is not in vain. Because the resurrection is real, the future is secure and magnificent.

> *Death has been swallowed up in the victory of the resurrection.*

23 Closing Remarks—1 Cor. 16:1–24

THREE-PART AGENDA

ICE-BREAKER
15 Minutes

BIBLE STUDY
30 Minutes

CARING TIME
15–45 Minutes

LEADER: Check page M7 of the center section for a good ice-breaker for this last session.

TO BEGIN THE BIBLE STUDY TIME
(Choose 1 or 2)

1. When you travel, do you like to plan things thoroughly, or just go with the flow?

2. Who is someone you would like to go visit that you haven't seen in a long time?

3. When you look toward the future, what are some of the plans you have?

READ SCRIPTURE & DISCUSS
(If you don't have time for all the questions in this section, conclude the Bible Study [30 min.] by answering question #7.)

1. How has this group, or someone in the group, been a blessing to you over the course of this study?

2. What kind of collection did Paul ask of the Corinthians? How do you feel about giving money? What compels you to give?

3. After receiving this letter, how do you think the Corinthians felt about Paul's plan to visit them? Beneath all his corrective instruction, how do you think Paul felt about the Corinthians?

The Collection for God's People

16 *Now about the collection for God's people: Do what I told the Galatian churches to do. ²On the first day of every week, each one of you should set aside a sum of money in keeping with his income, saving it up, so that when I come no collections will have to be made. ³Then, when I arrive, I will give letters of introduction to the men you approve and send them with your gift to Jerusalem. ⁴If it seems advisable for me to go also, they will accompany me.*

Personal Requests

⁵After I go through Macedonia, I will come to you—for I will be going through Macedonia. ⁶Perhaps I will stay with you awhile, or even spend the winter, so that you can help me on my journey, wherever I go. ⁷I do not want to see you now and make only a passing visit; I hope to spend some time with you, if the Lord permits. ⁸But I will stay on at Ephesus until Pentecost, ⁹because a great door for effective work has opened to me, and there are many who oppose me.

¹⁰If Timothy comes, see to it that he has nothing to fear while he is with you, for he is carrying on the work of the Lord, just as I am. ¹¹No one, then, should refuse to accept him. Send him on his way in peace so that he may return to me. I am expecting him along with the brothers. ¹²Now about our brother Apollos: I strongly urged him to go to you with the brothers. He was quite unwilling to go now, but he will go when he has the opportunity.

¹³Be on your guard; stand firm in the faith; be men of courage; be strong. ¹⁴Do everything in love.

¹⁵You know that the household of Stephanas were the first converts in Achaia, and they have devoted themselves to the service of the saints. I urge you, brothers, ¹⁶to submit to such as these and to everyone who joins in the work, and labors at it. ¹⁷I was glad when Stephanas, Fortunatus and Achaicus arrived, because they have supplied what was lacking from you. ¹⁸For they refreshed my spirit and yours also. Such men deserve recognition.

4. How would you feel if, like Timothy, Paul was sending you to this church?

5. Which of Paul's concluding exhortations in verses 13–14 do you most want to apply in your life: Be on your guard? Stand firm in the faith? Have courage? Be strong? Do everything in love?

6. What was the key thing you learned in this study of 1 Corinthians?

7. On a scale of 1 (baby steps) to 10 (giant leaps), how has your relationship with Christ progressed over the last five months?

CARING TIME

(Answer all the questions below, then take prayer requests and close with prayer.)

1. What will you remember most about this group?

2. What has the group decided to do next? What is the next step for you personally?

3. How would you like the group to continue to pray for you?

Notes—1 Corinthians 16:1–24

Summary. Paul ends his epistle by attending to a series of "housekeeping matters": the collection for the poor in Jerusalem, his own travel plans and those of his colleagues, the question of Stephanas' ministry in the church, and greetings from various friends. The abrupt transition from the heights of theology phrased in the language of praise to the mundane details of everyday life is typical of Paul's writing.

16:1 *Now about.* Paul deals with another question which they asked in their letter (7:1; 8:1; 12:1).

the collection. When in Jerusalem, Paul had agreed to help support the poor there (Gal. 2:10). In this way, the Gentile and the Jewish wings of the church would be bound together in a new fashion. This is a voluntary collection to be given to the mother church in Jerusalem. The word Paul uses for this collection is *logia*, which means "an extra collection."

16:2 *On the first day.* Sunday, when Christians met for worship.

set aside. Paul is not calling for a collection to be taken each Sunday for his purpose. Rather, he asks individual Christians to set aside funds on their own.

no collections will have to be made. Paul hoped that each person would have a sum of money set aside, ready to hand over when he came, so that he would not have to bother with the time-consuming process of taking a collection.

16:3 *letters of introduction.* A common way by which a person was commended to another person or community.

men you approve. The Corinthians would select their own messengers, so as to diffuse any possible misunderstanding about why Paul was taking up the collection, and how it would be used.

16:4 Acts 20:1–21:17 describes a journey by Paul from Greece to Jerusalem, and even though no Corinthians are named directly as traveling companions, it seems likely that this was so (see Rom. 15:26).

16:5–9 Paul now describes his further travel plans. He is writing from Ephesus (v. 8), where he plans to stay awhile since he is having a fruitful ministry there.

16:10–11 Timothy's trip to Corinth is in doubt ("If Timothy comes"—v. 10). Why Timothy is afraid is not clear. Perhaps as Paul's assistant, he fears a hostile welcome from the unpredictable Corinthians.

16:12 The Corinthians evidently want a visit from Apollos. Paul informs them that Apollos is not willing to visit them yet. Perhaps he and Paul have decided that since one "party" is rallying around his name, the cause of unity would be aided if he did not visit.

16:13 *Be on your guard.* This expression is often used to urge watchfulness in terms of the Second Coming. "Be alert to the events of the last days, lest they catch you unaware," seems to be Paul's admonition.

16:14 In chapter 13, Paul has defined this way of love for them.

16:15–16 Paul calls upon the Corinthians to recognize the ministry of Stephanas and his family. These people have given themselves over to the service of their fellow believers. Furthermore, Paul calls upon the Corinthians to follow these, their natural leaders—no doubt a most difficult request for the stubborn, proud Corinthians.

16:16 *submit.* "The verb 'submit' is used only here in the New Testament to refer to the relationship of a Christian community to those who labor among them. Although this could possibly mean to be in submission to them in some form of obedience, both the context and the similar passage in 1 Thessalonians 5:12–13 suggest rather that it means 'submission in the sense of voluntary yielding in love' ..." (Fee).

to such as these and to everyone who joins in the work. In fact, it is not just to the family of Stephanas that the Corinthians should look for leadership. Other emerging leaders ought also to be followed in a spirit of submission, for the sake of ministry in general.

16:17 These three supplied Paul with some of the information he has about the Corinthian church. While Stephanas is also presumably mentioned in verse 15, this seems to be the only reference to Fortunatus and Achaicus.

16:18 *recognition.* Here are more of the natural leaders in the church (who presumably have the potential for bringing order out of the chaos in Corinth, if they are allowed to do so by the rest of the church).

16:19 *Aquila and Priscilla.* They are now, apparently, in Ephesus. Paul met them first in Corinth, where they journeyed after Jews were expelled from Rome. Aquila and Priscilla were (presumably) quite wealthy, since they were business people. They traveled freely, and they had a house in Ephesus—where the (or a) church met.

16:20 *a holy kiss.* This was a custom used in the early church as part of the worship service. Kisses were a common form of greeting in biblical times.

16:21 Paul normally dictated his letters and then authenticated them by writing a final comment in his own handwriting.

16:22 *a curse be on him.* Some in Corinth had pronounced a curse upon Jesus (12:3). Paul reverses that here and calls for God's judgment upon those who fail to love Jesus and, by implication, follow him. The Lord is then invoked as a witness to the judgment.

Come, O Lord. This is an Aramaic expression, *Maranatha,* transliterated by Paul into Greek (see also Rev. 22:20). This was an expression used by the early Christians that Christ would soon return. The Lord's return would mark the moment when the curse on those who had refused to love him would be put into effect.

16:23–24 He concludes his letter in typical fashion. Paul began by thanking God for the Corinthians (1:1–9), and he ends his letter in the same spirit. They are beloved brothers and sisters in the Lord, despite all the hard things he has had to say to them. In fact, it is because he loved them that he wrote what he did.

16:24 *My love to all of you.* This is unique to all of Paul's letters.

Acknowledgments

While use has been made of the standard exegetical tools, two books in particular warrant special note. First is C. K. Barrett's fine commentary, *The First Epistle to the Corinthians*, New York, Harper and Row, 1966; and *Corinthians: A Study Guide* written by Gordon Fee, Brussels, Belgium: International Correspondence Institute, 1979. His commentary, *The First Epistle to the Corinthians* (The New International Commentary on the New Testament), Grand Rapids, MI: Wm. B. Eerdmans Publishing Co., 1987 had not been completed when the original notes were written. Some reference was made to this fine volume, however, in the revision of the notes for this edition.

Occasional use was made of *The First Epistle of Paul to the Corinthians* by Leon Morris (Tyndale New Testament Commentaries), London: The Tyndale Press, 1958; *The Letters to the Corinthians* by William Barclay (The Daily Study Bible), Edinburgh: The Saint Andrews Press, 1954; *I and II Corinthians* by Margaret Thrall (The Cambridge Bible Commentary of the New English Bible), Cambridge: The University Press, 1965; *A Critical and Exegetical Commentary on the First Epistle of St. Paul to the Corinthians* by Robertson and Plummer (The International Critical Commentary), Edinburgh: T. & T. Clark, 1914; *I Corinthians: Challenge to Maturity* by Marilyn Kuntz and Catherine Schell (Neighborhood Bible Studies), Wheaton: Tyndale House Publishers, 1973.

Caring Time Notes

Caring Time Notes